THE SECRET OF EMOTIONAL INTELLIGENCE

A COMPREHENSIVE GUIDE TO REDUCE STRESS, ENHANCE PERSONAL AND PROFESSIONAL INTERACTION, AND ELEVATE LEADERSHIP

G. GAGLIARDI.

TABLE OF CONTENTS

Introduction   5

1. F-FUNDAMENTALS   11
   Introduction to Emotional Intelligence   11
   Importance of EI in Everyday Life   15
   The Role of EI in Effective Leadership   18
   Real-World Examples and Case Studies   23

2. O-OBSERVATION   27
   Defining Self-Awareness and Its Significance   28
   Techniques for Self-Assessment and
   Reflection   32
   How Leaders Use Self-Awareness to Make
   Better Decisions   38
   Exercises and Activities for Improving Self-
   Awareness   41

3. C-COMMUNICATION   47
   Importance of Listening in Communication   48
   Principles of Active Listening   51
   Active Listening Anywhere   54
   Nonverbal Communication in Active
   Listening   57
   Tips and Exercises for Enhancing Listening
   Abilities   59

4. U-UNDERSTANDING   65
   The Essence of Empathy in EI   66
   Empathy's Role in Leadership   69
   Empathy in Personal Relationships   72
   Activities to Develop Empathetic Skills   75

5. S-SLOW DOWN   83

   The Drawbacks of Impulsive Reactions   84

   The Power of Pausing and Thoughtful
   Responding   88

   Pausing and Decision-Making   91

   Techniques to Practice Taking a Moment
   Before Reacting   95

6. E-EASE   99

   The Impact of Stress on EI   100

   Stress Management Techniques Beneficial for
   Everyone   103

   How Managing Stress Enhances Leadership
   Capability   108

   Quick and Long-Term Stress-Relief Methods   110

7. D-DEEP RELATIONSHIPS   115

   EI in Interpersonal Relationships   116

   How EI Skills Improve Work Relations and
   Team Dynamics   120

   Guidelines for Using EI to Maintain and
   Improve Relationships   125

   Conclusion   135
   References   141

INTRODUCTION

Have you ever felt surprised by how others depicted you? Perhaps you have had a deep conversation with one of your colleagues after work and found out they don't perceive you as you think. You might have thought they made jokes about you and found you boring when, in reality, they always appreciated your sense of humor and intelligence. If you're in a relationship, maybe you have argued more than once with your significant other. Have you ever felt shocked by their words and reacted impulsively? Maybe they told you something like, "You never think about what I want and need!" and you might have become upset. In your heart, you know you listen to your partner and care for their needs and wants, so you get angry because they don't seem to understand you.

Researchers have studied emotional intelligence (EI) in the workplace and found that 90% of top performers achieved high results in EI while only 20% of bottom performers did (Bradberry, 2014). Other studies have found that only 36% of people can correctly identify their emotions as they occur (*What Is Emotional Intelligence and 4 Ways to Improve It*, 2018). Emotional intelligence is the ability to properly label, understand, and express our emotions and thoughts and correctly assess others'. You might believe many people are able to identify their emotions, but that's a rare skill only a few possess. Among them, top performers or people who achieve great results at work are the ones who show higher levels of EI. Consequently, this skill is connected with success and better performance at work.

Emotional intelligence is key to feeling happy and satisfied in all aspects of your life. If you lack such skill, you might notice some recurrent patterns, like constantly feeling overwhelmed and stressed or suffering from burnout. Consequently, your relationships with the people around you, your work, and your mental and physical health are negatively affected. You might also feel fatigued, lack motivation to accomplish daily tasks, and have negative feelings toward yourself, what you do, and what happens in your life. In other words, you see the glass half empty and believe you'll never succeed. You wonder why you react in unhealthy ways and can't control your impulses, and you feel like you're not able to stay calm and face difficult situations with a peaceful mind. In addition, you might ask yourself why you often don't manage to make the right decisions for you.

If you lack emotional intelligence, you might also struggle to communicate your feelings and emotions properly. It's possible you have noticed conflicts and misunderstandings easily arise in your personal and professional life. You might feel like nobody understands you or listens to you or struggle to occupy leadership positions like being responsible for a team at work. You might believe people don't listen to you and you're not able to take the lead, thus letting others do as they prefer. The main effect of all the above difficulties might be that you're not satisfied with your relationships, especially the most meaningful ones.

If you recognize yourself in the above statements, you mustn't feel alone or different from everyone else. As statistics show, EI is a rare skill. If you wish to improve your communication and relationship skills and increase your mental and physical health, you have the power to do it. In fact, you can learn to become more emotionally intelligent. Emotions are at the basis of any interactions with others and our ability to be aware of who we are, what we feel, and how we think. Once you become better at expressing and understanding your emotions and others, you'll feel happier and more satisfied in all aspects of your life.

Thanks to *The Secret of Emotional Intelligence: A Comprehensive Guide to Reduce Stress, Enhance Personal and Professional Interaction, and Elevate Leadership*, you'll learn to become more self-aware. Therefore, you'll be able to correctly identify your emotions as they occur and express how you feel to others. You'll also discover how to control your impulses and change your reactions to difficult situations, thus living a more balanced life. Consequently, you'll be able to pause before making a decision, evaluate the situation, and do the right thing. In addition, you'll learn the secret to improving your communication skills: listening. When you learn how to properly listen to others, you'll enhance your relationships. You'll find practical techniques to manage stress and tackle daily challenges without feeling overwhelmed. Finally, you'll improve your leadership skills, thus enhancing your ability to handle teams at work, solve conflicts, and create a more harmonious work environment.

In this book, you'll discover the potential of FOCUSED, an acronym that stands for Fundamentals, Observation, Communication, Understanding, Slowing down, Ease, and Deep relationships. Each chapter will focus on a different element of the FOCUSED framework. Chapter 1 will provide a complete overview of the topic of emotional intelligence and why it's important in your everyday life. Chapter 2 will analyze the concept of self-awareness, and Chapter 3 will teach you how to practice active listening and improve your nonverbal skills. Chapter 4 will discuss empathy, which is fundamental to boosting your relationships. Chapter 5 will focus on impulsive reactions and how to take a break before acting or making an important decision. Chapter 6 will teach you techniques to manage stress in your daily life and Chapter 7 will provide useful tips to enhance your relationships. Each chapter will contain a theoretical and a practical part that will allow you to put into practice what you learn easily.

This book doesn't just explain the what and why of emotional intelligence but also dives into the "how" by using a specific framework—FOCUSED. After reading it, you'll clearly understand what EI is and all the different tools you can use in your daily life to improve. You'll be able to apply the information you'll find immediately and in all contexts of your life. You'll move from simply reacting to life events and the things people say and do to you to thoughtful responding. Basically, you'll lead a more fulfilling and balanced life.

1

F-FUNDAMENTALS

 Emotional intelligence accounts for 80% of career success.

— DANIEL GOLEMAN

You might have heard about emotional intelligence at least once and thought it was just a buzzword with no real effect on your daily life. As you'll discover in this book, EI is much more than that. It's your key to success in your personal and professional life. In this chapter, you'll learn what EI entails, its effects and significance on your daily life, how it impacts leadership skills, and concrete examples of how it manifests.

INTRODUCTION TO EMOTIONAL INTELLIGENCE

Emotional intelligence is also identified with the acronym EQ, which stands for emotional quotient (Cherry, 2023e). It's the ability to properly use your emotions to communicate with the people around you and relate to them. In other words, you understand and manage your emotions effectively. At the same time, you're also able to identify and influence the emotions of others (Landry, 2019). Researchers John Mayer and Peter Salovey coined the term in 1990, but it became popular only thanks to psychologist Daniel Goleman. Before researchers started talking about EI, the most popular concept was cognitive intelligence (IQ), which was considered essential to succeed in life. Nowadays, many scholars agree that EI is much more important and a more effective predictor of success. Psychologist Daniel Goleman suggested that the main trait all effective leaders share is emotional intelligence. Research has confirmed that employees with higher levels of EI are more likely to solve conflicts more easily, respond with empathy, and stay calm under pressure (Landry, 2019).

Emotional intelligence is a complex skill that includes four core components: Self-awareness, social awareness, self-management, and relationship management (Landry, 2019). Self-awareness indicates being aware of yourself, your strengths and weaknesses, and your emotions. Knowing yourself is paramount to improving interactions with others, reducing stress, and increasing motivation. Interestingly, researcher Tasha Eurich tested the levels of self-awareness on a sample and discovered that 95% defined themselves as self-aware but only 10–15% could actually be identified as such. This means most people think they know themselves, but in reality, they don't. Therefore, they're not aware of their reactions, how they interact with others, and how they express their emotions and thoughts. Social awareness indicates the ability to correctly assess how others feel and social dynamics. If you're socially aware, you can understand when you're not welcome in a social context, how members of the same group interact, and how others perceive you. Social awareness allows you to boost your relationships by understanding what others might want from you and what you want from them (Landry, 2019).

Self-management consists of being able to control yourself when things don't go as planned (Landry, 2019). In other words, you properly manage your emotions in stressful situations. To understand self-management, you must know the difference between reaction and response first. A reaction is impulsive and might lead to negative effects for you and the people around you, while a response is a thoughtful answer to a difficult circumstance. If you're responsive, you're able to take a break, analyze the situation, and do whatever you need to calm down before saying or doing anything. If you possess self-management, you respond rather than react to stressful events. Relationship management is the ability to influence and mentor others and properly solve conflicts. If you effectively manage your relationships, you know how to achieve your goals without taking advantage of others because you respect them and appreciate their successes. You accept feedback and prefer collaborating to tackle problems. In addition, you don't avoid conflicts but try to solve them effectively because you know open communication is fundamental and must be promoted. If you keep your problems to yourself, they might become bigger and cause more arguments and misunderstandings (Landry, 2019).

EI is not a trait but a skill. A trait is something you have that characterizes you and is quite fixed throughout your life. For instance, introversion is a trait because you can be introverted or not and you'll always be like that. Obviously, you can become a bit more extroverted if you work on your social and communication skills, but you won't transform from a person who avoids all parties to someone who never misses a weekend out with friends to have fun. Conversely, EI is a skill because we can all possess it if we work on it and practice specific activities and techniques. If you want to become more emotionally intelligent, you just need to invest time and energy in it.

To get used to becoming aware of your emotions, start by paying attention to your feelings and behaviors. Keeping a journal might make the task easier. In your daily life, you might feel stressed and overwhelmed and lack the time to think about how you feel and how you behave. You might even lose touch with your emotions and not be able to recognize your reactions. To become more aware of your feelings, dedicate a few minutes every day to take a break and reflect on them. For example, when you wake up in the morning, wait for a few seconds before getting out of bed to think about how you feel. You can analyze your physical sensations and where your emotions come from in your body, like your stomach, head, or heart. Then, repeat the same activity at the end of the day before going to bed. You reflect on what happened and try to relive the emotions you felt and analyze them. You can also think about your physical reactions and how they might have affected others. If you had an important conversation with one of your colleagues or your superiors, consider how you felt and what you did before, during, and after it. After some time, you'll get used to analyzing your thoughts and behaviors and you'll do it naturally. At that point, start repeating to yourself that you're the only one responsible for your feelings. If you feel stressed and overwhelmed, it's because you choose to feel that way, not because of external events or other people. Once you accept it, you're more likely to take a pause when you need it and control your reactions.

IMPORTANCE OF EI IN EVERYDAY LIFE

You might wonder how the four core components of emotional intelligence influence your everyday life. If you're highly self-aware and socially aware and can manage yourself and your relationships, you can improve your workplace. Have you ever worked in a toxic environment? You might not have a clear idea of what "toxic" entails, but still, some memories come to your mind. For instance, you might have worked for a company where you didn't feel free to express your opinion. Your superiors might have made all the decisions and fostered competition, thus making you fight with your coworkers. Many leaders believe they must punish their employees if they make a mistake and maintain high levels of competition to push people to work more and better. However, they often achieve the opposite because they encourage a toxic workplace. If a leader is emotionally intelligent, they know they must listen to all their employees' concerns and let them participate in the decision-making process. This doesn't mean to give them all the power but to make them feel valued and appreciated. In the end, the leader is the one who will make a decision.

Emotionally intelligent leaders promote resilience when changes occur and new initiatives are introduced. They support their employees in understanding what they should do and show them how. In addition, they foster flexibility in the sense that they help employees adapt to change. A sign of a healthy workplace is that coworkers are happy to spend time together, even after office hours. As an emotionally intelligent employee or leader, you can promote cooperation and a positive environment by collaborating with your colleagues and creating deep connections. You can take advantage of not only your strengths and weaknesses but also those of others. If you notice one of your coworkers is often quiet but has innovative ideas, you help them express their opinion. If you notice someone bossing around, you don't promote that behavior and try to allow everyone to make mistakes and have a say. Moreover, you stick to your values and show your passions and motivation, thus inspiring others to do the same.

Becoming emotionally intelligent can have positive effects on your relationships, too. For example, you can understand when it's better to express your opinion and when it's not. Even if you love your partner or best friend, you might feel irritated by certain behaviors they engage in unintentionally. They might do something that makes you feel upset and you might feel the urge to say something to make them stop. If you're emotionally intelligent, you evaluate the situation and wonder if you do the right thing by pointing out their behavior. You reflect before acting and consider their point of view.

You might understand they don't behave that way intention-ally to make you feel irritated and their actions don't provoke any major negative effects in your life. Therefore, you might decide to simply let go and move on with your life. At the same time, you know when to stand up for your-self and when your partner or best friend has crossed some serious boundaries.

Research has found that emotional intelligence can improve your life in many ways (Houston, 2019). It helps you form and develop meaningful connections by increasing your empathy, encouraging you to cooperate, developing affec-tionate and more satisfying relationships, and boosting your social skills. Studies have found that those who exhibit higher levels of EI are more likely to experience gratifying and successful interpersonal relationships. At the same time, EI has incredible effects on your physical health because it reduces chronic stress, the risk of heart problems, and susceptibility to viruses; it even increases your probability of healing from wounds and injuries (Houston, 2019). EI can help you become happier and increase your overall well-being.

Nowadays, companies and leaders are becoming aware of the importance and positive effects of emotional intelligence in the workplace (Duggal, 2018). Until recently, they believed emotions had to be left outside of work and the only essen-tial thing was cognitive intelligence and the ability to complete tasks efficiently. In reality, emotions have always been present in the workplace but they've been neglected or hidden, thus increasing negative feelings like resentment and frustration. At the same time, working in teams has become a priority and forced many people to collaborate even if they don't possess the appropriate relationship and communication skills. For all these reasons, EI has become increasingly important and can foster a positive work environment. In fact, research has found that highly emotionally intelligent leaders have happier employees who tend to stay longer and put more effort into their jobs, thus increasing productivity and reducing attrition rates (Duggal, 2018). Finally, EI helps solve conflicts effectively. If you have low levels of this skill, you might provoke arguments because you don't know how to control yourself or don't consider others' points of view. Conversely, if you have high levels, you can handle arguments among your employees or coworkers and avoid them in the future (Houston, 2019). The ability to solve conflicts properly has many advantages not only in the workplace but also in your personal life.

THE ROLE OF EI IN EFFECTIVE LEADERSHIP

Emotional intelligence is an essential skill for leaders. Obviously, technical skills are paramount: If you don't possess the right qualities, you can't manage your company. However, EI is just as important because you must manage relationships in the workplace effectively. If you excel at your job but can't collaborate and communicate with others, your professional skills are useless and won't help you grow your company. A lack of EI might have more far-reaching consequences than a lack of technical skills, like lower employee engagement (Landry, 2019).

As a leader, increasing your levels of EI can have numerous benefits for your company and employees (Emeritus, 2023). First, you foster stronger connections by being empathetic and understanding. You create a safe environment where employees feel appreciated and understood when they need your help. You listen to their points of view and try to put yourself in their shoes and reach a compromise that can benefit everyone. In turn, your empathy promotes loyalty and trust, thus making your employees feel more engaged in their daily tasks. They're more willing to share their ideas and work toward a common goal that they consider valuable. In other words, EI develops an inclusive and supportive environment (Emeritus, 2023).

Moreover, emotionally intelligent leaders promote clear and open communication with their employees. They actively listen and know how to provide constructive feedback without criticizing or demeaning others. They're also role models employees follow happily. In fact, emotionally intelligent leaders share their passions, motivations, and goals and try to instill them in the people around them. Therefore, they do their best to stimulate others and explain their decisions so that everyone understands the main goals. This way, team members feel excited about what they do and have a sense of purpose. Emotionally intelligent leaders not only provide useful feedback but also know how to receive it from their employees. They don't feel attacked or react defensively if team members notice one or more shortcomings. Conversely, they value their feedback and do their best to improve. When they have to make a decision, they always consider how it might impact their company and employees, thus making the best choices for everyone and increasing the possibility of success (Emeritus, 2023).

Last but not least, emotionally intelligent leaders promote a positive organizational culture. If you show empathy and self-awareness, your employees are more likely to do the same. As they feel appreciated and understood, they deepen their connections, collaborate more, and feel more empathetic toward each other. They understand they don't have to compete because they all pursue the same goal. Such an organizational culture not only boosts employee retention but also attracts top talents who realize they're appreciated. This way, your company becomes more cohesive, innovative, and, ultimately, successful. The more your employees are satisfied, the more your organization grows (Emeritus, 2023).

You might struggle to imagine emotionally intelligent leaders because you think about strong, fierce, cold, and distant ones who never share power or accept feedback from others. They simply go their own way and follow their rules without considering other people's opinions and emotions. However, past and recent history provides plenty of examples of leaders who promote emotional intelligence and use it in their workplace. For example, Abraham Lincoln can be considered the most emotionally intelligent President of the US (*Emotional Intelligence in Leaders: Real Life Examples*, 2016). He always listened to his advisers but ultimately, made his own decisions, always keeping his citizens' emotions in mind. He promoted emancipation and refused to punish the Confederacy even when everyone was advising the contrary. Abraham Lincoln valued people's emotions and dignity more than anything else (*Emotional Intelligence in Leaders: Real Life Examples*, 2016).

More recently, the CEO of Microsoft, Satya Nadella, showed emotional intelligence to his engineers (Morey, 2018). They worked on a Twitter bot named Tay that was supposed to facilitate communication online but was used by Twitter users to share profane and racist comments. In less than 16 hours since its release, the project had to be shut down. As you might guess, it was an embarrassing failure for Microsoft and engineers felt mortified. However, Satya Nadella sent them an email reminding them that he has their back and encouraging them to keep learning and improving. Moreover, he fostered a positive environment by telling staffers to take criticism in the right way. In general, Satya Nadella believes a leader shouldn't prove power by fear but by understanding and showing empathy to their employees (Morey, 2018). This is a striking example of how emotionally intelligent leaders work.

If you don't perform formal or managerial roles, like CEO, you might believe developing emotional intelligence to become an effective leader doesn't concern you. Most people are convinced only leaders should possess leadership skills and they're not essential for all other people. However, we should all aim to develop such skills—even if we're employees and will perform the same position for the rest of our lives. Leadership is part of our routine and we need leadership skills to take responsibility for our actions, take the initiative, impact others positively, build deep connections, and be empathetic. If you develop your leadership skills, you take charge of your life and feel empowered. You realize you can follow your path and can grow as an individual. You become proactive and aim at making choices that align with your values. In addition, working on your leadership skills is strictly connected with developing essential qualities and values like integrity, honesty, resilience, and accountability.

Building leadership skills also allows you to forge positive relationships. Leadership involves interacting with other people, meaning you must develop excellent communication skills and foster collaboration, which is paramount in all types of relationships. If you improve your leadership skills, you're also able to solve problems by thinking critically and evaluating various options. Therefore, you tackle challenges with a positive and solution-oriented attitude. Have you ever found yourself in a difficult situation and felt paralyzed because you didn't know what to do? Building your leadership skills can help you overcome everyday obstacles. Finally, they allow you to make a difference in the world by instilling your values and thoughts into others. If you show honesty, integrity, dynamism, and other qualities, you might encourage others to do the same. Let's say you develop a strong work ethic and show your colleagues you put effort into every task you accomplish. If they notice you achieve great results and feel satisfied with what you do, they're likely to develop a strong work ethic, too. The same is true in all aspects of your life, even your romantic relationships and friendships.

REAL-WORLD EXAMPLES AND CASE STUDIES

Let's look at some practical ways in which people can use EI in their daily lives. Let's say you're the CEO of a company that is in rapid expansion and recruiting many new specialists. Every two months, you have scheduled meetings with the staff and employees to discuss current issues. You might hate such meetings because you just have to sit there, listening to your staff complaining about things like having more space in their offices. At some point, you might decide to switch off your head during the meetings and think about something else while maintaining a cheerful face. However, you realize that more and more employees are starting to leave the company and business is not going well (*Case Study - 27: Emotional Intelligence in Corporate Offices*, 2022). What can you do to make sure your employees are satisfied and keep working at your company?

If you lack emotional intelligence, you can decide not to do anything and keep sitting through the meetings without helping your employees. This way, you seriously risk losing all your staff, decreasing productivity, and letting your company fail. If you possess high levels of EI, you understand you must do something to protect your company and make your employees happy. Therefore, you start analyzing the situation. You realize the company recruited many new workers while maintaining the same offices. Consequently, the building has become overcrowded. At the same time, you're aware your attitude toward the meetings doesn't help your employees feel understood and appreciated. You must handle the crisis efficiently, avoid conflicts between you and your staff, and make an effective decision promptly. You realize you mainly have two options (*Case Study - 27: Emotional Intelligence in Corporate Offices*, 2022).

The most evident solution is to find a better and bigger workplace. However, it might require time and increase negative feelings among employees. For these reasons, you must not only elaborate on the long-term goal of finding a better place but also on short-term ones, like making sure all spaces are clean or optimizing offices. In addition, you must put all your effort into listening to your employees and making them understand you care about them and their work conditions. Therefore, you stop switching off during meetings and show others you're present and attentive. You also show them you do your best to make some progress and have a new place ready as soon as possible. Alternatively, you can rethink work conditions and offer employees the opportunity to work from home. For instance, you can decide that 50% of your staff can stay in the office while the remaining 50% stays at home. Remote working provides various alternatives and allows you to hire new staff without having to look for a bigger and probably more expensive place. At the same time, some coworkers might take advantage of remote working to spend more time with their families and feel more relaxed (*Case Study - 27: Emotional Intelligence in Corporate Offices*, 2022).

If you ever find yourself in a situation similar to the above case study, you must consider your feelings and goals, the objectives you want to pursue inside your company, and your employees' well-being. If your staff keeps complaining, something's certainly wrong, so be proactive and look into the situation to improve the work conditions. Top performers prefer working in a place where they feel appreciated and valued and don't struggle to find another job. Therefore, you must do your best to attract and keep them. If you don't value your employees, your company is more likely to fail.

Practicing emotional intelligence can also improve your personal life. Let's say you've been married for years with your significant other. Conflicts about small things keep arising and your partner complains about being ignored or misunderstood by you. You might easily get angry and extend arguments by highlighting all the things you do for them and they don't do for you. In the long term, you might hinder your relationship. If you have high levels of EI, you accept something's wrong and become proactive. You analyze the situation by discussing it with your significant other and considering that you've been together for quite some time. You both realize you enjoyed some activities you've stopped practicing together, like going for a hike or exploring new cities close to you. You reflect on what you and your partner want and need and what's best for your relationship. You understand you need to change something and put effort into dedicating some time to yourselves by taking a walk around the neighborhood or doing day trips during the weekends.

In this chapter, we thoroughly analyzed the concept of emotional intelligence, which is the ability to understand, label, and express our emotions and recognize others' feelings. It's a complex skill that is composed of four different components: Self-awareness, social awareness, relationship management, and self-management. Next, we discussed all the benefits that becoming emotionally intelligent can have in our daily lives. We realized EI can improve our workplaces and relationships with others. Then, we focused on how this ability can help leaders become more effective and improve the leadership skills in all of us. In fact, we don't need to be a leader in our workplace to value leadership skills. Finally, we looked at two case studies to understand the difference between reacting without emotional intelligence and responding with empathy to difficult situations. Now that we understand the basics, it's time to dive deep into the first key aspect and core component: self-awareness.

2

O-OBSERVATION

> *The first step toward change is awareness. If you want to get from where you are to where you want to be, you have to start by becoming aware of the choices that lead you away from your desired destination.*
>
> — DARREN HARDY

The first step to improving your relationships and decision-making is to become aware of yourself. If you don't know who you are, you can't manage your interactions with others and make the right choices. Becoming aware of yourself isn't a luxury but necessary to live a more fulfilling and successful life. Without self-awareness, we're like ships without a compass, aimlessly sailing through life. In this chapter, you'll discover what self-awareness is and how it impacts your daily life. Next, you'll learn some simple and useful techniques to become more self-aware and how renowned leaders use self-awareness to make the right decisions. Finally, you'll find some practical exercises you can do right now to test your level of self-awareness and improve.

DEFINING SELF-AWARENESS AND ITS SIGNIFICANCE

We already introduced the concept of self-awareness in the previous chapter but didn't explain it in detail. To understand what it means to be self-aware, think about toddlers and how they interact with the world. Studies have found that infants are aware that they're different beings from others and that they constitute an entity on their own (Cherry, 2023c). In other words, they're aware their parents are separate from them, like the rest of the people they interact with. An easy experiment to understand if toddlers are aware of themselves is to place them in front of a mirror and see what they do. If they try to reach their nose or other parts of their body, they understand they're seeing their image reflected in the mirror. If they touch the glass, they don't recognize themselves, so they're not self-aware (Cherry, 2023c).

The most basic form of self-awareness corresponds to differentiation, which means that a baby is aware of their own image reflected in a mirror (Cherry, 2023c). However, self-awareness is a complicated concept that involves different layers. If you're self-aware, you recognize not only yourself in the mirror, but also the behaviors you engage in, features that distinguish yourself from the rest of the people, and how others perceive you. In other words, self-awareness is the ability to understand and identify all the elements that make you, you, like your beliefs, values, habits, actions, emotions, and thoughts. Being self-aware is not a permanent state but a concept that emerges in certain moments of your life. For instance, you can be aware that you hurt someone with your words or that your friends don't agree with you. However, you can't constantly be aware of yourself and how others see you (Cherry, 2023c).

Self-awareness is so complex that it can be divided into two types: private and public (Cherry, 2023c). Private self-awareness is the ability to understand who you are and be aware of your thoughts, emotions, strengths, and weaknesses. It can be as easy as realizing you feel hungry because your stomach lurches or more complex, like recognizing when you're about to get anxious because your heart beats faster than usual. If you possess private self-awareness, you know what you can and can't do, what situations make you feel comfortable, and what events provoke stress in you. Developing this skill is essential to knowing yourself better and improving your relationships. If you know who you are, you can achieve your goals more easily, take advantage of your skills, and avoid challenging situations. Private self-awareness helps you make the right choices for you.

Public self-awareness concerns your relationships with others and if you can correctly assess how people see you (Cherry, 2023c). Most people show public self-awareness when they know they're being watched and evaluated, so they pay attention to what they say and do to satisfy the observers. In fact, the main disadvantage of public self-awareness is that it can hinder the possibility of showing our true selves to please others. If you possess high levels of public self-awareness, you know what others want from you and what social norms you should adhere to. Consequently, you do your best to abide by them and satisfy people's expectations. If they expect you to answer "Yes" to their requests, then you're going to say "Yes," even if that's not what you want and it won't improve your life in any way. At the same time, public self-awareness can help you understand different situations and social dynamics. You're aware when people don't like certain behaviors you engage in or when they value your opinions and consider you important in their lives.

How does self-awareness apply to real life? Let's imagine you feel stressed because you often submit work projects on the day of the deadline or even later. You feel like there's nothing you can do about it and you're just too busy to be able to submit projects on time or in advance. If you practice self-awareness, you start reflecting on your thoughts and actions. You might realize everyone is busy, you're not the only one who has many responsibilities, and your colleagues manage to submit projects earlier than you. This means there might be a problem with the way you manage your workload. After careful evaluation, you might find out you tend to procrastinate until the last minute and you're not truly busy, but spend your time being distracted by things that aren't as important as your job. Consequently, you proactively look for solutions to reduce procrastination and maintain your focus on your projects.

The same can happen with your relationships. You might complain about the fact that your partner doesn't show as much affection and love as you do with them. You might discuss it frequently and end up arguing. After working on your self-awareness, you start wondering if you're part of the problem. You might acknowledge you're the first one not to notice or give importance to what your significant other does for you. You might also realize you assume they don't show affection purposely because they don't want to see you happy. You decide to discuss your thoughts with them and do something about it. You might start sharing your feelings and what you want from a relationship. Then, you might propose solutions and put your ideas into practice.

As you might have already guessed, becoming more self-aware can have many benefits in your professional and personal life (Ackerman, 2020). First, self-awareness boosts the acceptance of yourself, your strengths, and your weaknesses. You acknowledge you make mistakes as everyone does and you can improve. You're proactive and aim at growing as an individual. Second, self-awareness allows you to make the right choices based on what you want and need. Third, it increases your levels of self-esteem and helps you see things from the perspective of others. This way, you enhance your relationships at work and in your personal life. Finally, self-awareness boosts your communication skills, raises your levels of self-confidence, makes you better at your job, and increases your job-related well-being (Ackerman, 2020). In general, self-awareness can improve the quality of your life and make you feel happier and more satisfied.

TECHNIQUES FOR SELF-ASSESSMENT AND REFLECTION

You can practice various techniques to enhance your self-awareness, as you'll learn in the next sections. If you want, you can try the following activities as you read.

Keep an Open Mind

Being open-minded is generally associated with avoiding prejudices and being tolerant, but it's a broader concept. If you're open-minded, you're willing to try new experiences, consider different perspectives, and actively look for information that can challenge your beliefs. You might believe open-mindedness means accepting all opinions, even if you disagree with someone. However, being open-minded doesn't exclude having hard stances about specific topics, as we all have them. If you're passionate about something, you can have a strong opinion and still respect what others believe. If you want to become more open-minded, you must become aware of the confirmation bias and keep it in mind when considering various perspectives. Confirmation bias consists of paying more attention to evidence that confirms our existing beliefs and discarding everything else. For instance, you might be convinced you have to have kids to be happy and surround yourself with people who have the same conception. However, reality might be different, as many couples are happy even if they don't have children. You must analyze your beliefs and accept they might not be right. To avoid confirmation biases, you can expand your social network, meet people from different backgrounds, and ask questions not only to others to understand their point of view but also to yourself to evaluate your ideas (Cherry, 2023d).

Be Mindful of Strengths and Weaknesses

To become more self-aware, you must know your strengths and weaknesses. First, you must reconsider your idea of weakness because nobody is truly weak—we just need to develop some skills. Don't think of your deficiencies as weaknesses but as areas of development. This way, you'll look at them from a positive and renowned perspective and will be able to work on them. Keep in mind that you have the power to improve because your "weaknesses" aren't permanent but can be improved. Your areas of growth might include your job, hobbies, personal life, goals, or mental and physical health. Remember, nobody's perfect, and you can't be good at everything. Sometimes, you just need to acknowledge that you can't excel at all skills and only have positive qualities. Then, you focus on your strengths and try to identify all the skills you already have. Don't be harsh on yourself; you'll surely have more qualities than you think. Next, write down all your strengths and weaknesses and ask for people's feedback. For instance, you could ask your best friend or significant other what strengths and weaknesses they think you have. This way, you can compare your results with what others tell you and see if they correspond.

Stay Focused

If you want to become more self-aware, you must also take control of your attention and stay focused. Many people don't manage to maintain their concentration because they get easily distracted, don't sleep well or enough, don't practice enough physical activity, or don't eat healthy (Chia, 2021). If you don't manage to maintain your focus, you can improve by following some easy tips. You can eliminate all distractions, like your phone or noise. You can also reduce multitasking by completing one task at a time. If you practice more activities at the same time, you don't concentrate on any of them. In addition, you can improve your sleep quality and try to exercise more often. Two counterintuitive tips you can follow are to choose to focus on the task you want to accomplish and take a break. You must remember you have the power to concentrate on what you want. Even if you get distracted, you can acknowledge it and do your best to start focusing again. Moreover, breaks can be helpful if you concentrate on the same task for a long time. In fact, our brains can't maintain the same level of focus for hours. You can simply think about something different, talk to someone, or move around. If you want to increase your focus, you can also try meditation and mindfulness, which are based on the idea of maintaining your concentration as much as you can in a particular exercise. We'll look at mindfulness more in-depth in Chapter 6.

Know Your Emotional Triggers

An emotional trigger is a situation, event, person, or object that provokes an unexpected and intense emotional response (Cooks-Campbell, 2023). Examples of triggers include traumas, negative past experiences, fears, stressful situations, change, and relationship issues. An example of an emotional trigger might be a professional who was ignored in their previous role and becomes overly aggressive when they find another job. It might also be a young adult who avoids social events because they felt isolated in similar past situations. To recognize your triggers, you must become aware of your physical and emotional reactions. Do you feel anxious and struggle to calm down? Do you feel your heart beating fast? Do you feel like you're not in control of your body and thoughts? Next, analyze the cause of your worries, like a major, underlying issue. Listen to yourself and your body and check your feelings. Once you've found your triggers, it's time to accept them and acknowledge everyone feels uncomfortable in stressful situations. Don't fight your feelings but recognize them and talk about them with someone you trust (Cooks-Campbell, 2023).

Embrace Your Intuition

You've probably heard about intuition or gut feeling many times in your life and doubt its existence. You might consider yourself a person who believes in science, facts, and evidence. Researchers have found that intuition is a real psychological process that helps us decide by using past experiences and unconscious cues from ourselves and the environment (Young, 2016). Many studies have tried to analyze intuition and discovered that participants were unconsciously aware of certain situations and hints before they became conscious of them. Therefore, intuition exists and can help you enhance your self-awareness. Following your intuition simply means paying attention to what happens within and outside of you. You just follow your instincts and let your emotions flow naturally, even the negative ones. You accept them and let them go. In addition, you pay attention to what happens around you and the people you connect with. You distinguish between those who help you develop your intuition and those who drain you. Then, you're able to end unhealthy relationships that don't help you improve. To embrace your gut feeling, you can also dedicate some time just to yourself and stay in solitude for a few moments.

Practice Self-Discipline

To become more self-aware, you must find the perfect balance between following your intuition and respecting rules. In fact, self-discipline is just as important as your gut feeling. Self-discipline is the ability to choose to adhere to certain behaviors and rules you want to follow (Wooll, 2022a). It allows you to feel in control of your life and decide to resist temptations, thus reducing anxiety, increasing happiness, and raising your probability of achieving your goals. To become more self-disciplined, you must work on your long-term goals. Think about where you want to be in one, two, five, or ten years, and write down your answers. Once you've found your long-term goal, you can reflect on the small steps or short-term goals you need to follow. Make to-do lists and action plans to prioritize your tasks and prepare a backup plan in case things don't go as you thought or you change your goals. You can also ask for an extra push from your loved ones to feel more accountable for your actions.

Apologize When Necessary

If you become self-aware, you can recognize when apologizing is important. An apology usually comes after a conflict arises or you make a mistake. However, you don't need to apologize for everything. When you make a mistake, you must ask yourself if you're the main person responsible or if it's out of your control. If you realize external, uncontrollable factors or other people caused your mistakes, then an apology isn't necessary. If you acknowledge you've made an error and you're the main person responsible, you might need to apologize—but not in all cases. If you notice your mistake and do something to improve the situation without anyone getting hurt or offended, then you don't have to apologize. If you realize your error impacted someone else's feelings, an apology is necessary. However, not all apologies are effective because you must use the right words to make the person offended understand you're truly sorry. It's important to acknowledge your actions hurt them, take responsibility, agree that you did something wrong, say you're sorry and you regret behaving like that, and promise you will improve or not repeat the same actions. You can also add an explanation for your behavior, but only after you've followed the above steps. Otherwise, the offended person might perceive your clarification as defensive or an excuse. An explanation can help heal a relationship by making the offended person understand the reasons behind your behavior and setting the groundwork for renovated trust and respect.

HOW LEADERS USE SELF-AWARENESS TO MAKE BETTER DECISIONS

Self-awareness is an essential skill all leaders should have. Below, you'll find renowned figures who use their self-awareness to make the right decisions for themselves and the people who believe in them.

Nelson Mandela

Nelson Mandela is undoubtedly one of the greatest leaders of all time and an inspiration for many of us. He died in 2013 and left an unforgettable mark in the world (Williams, 2018). He differed from Gandhi and Martin Luther King as he embraced more violent forms of protest, especially when he was a young activist. He always fought against racism and also spent 27 years in prison, which made him angry and resentful. Therefore, he was no different from any other person: He also had negative feelings and expressed them. However, he was able to go beyond them to realize he had the power to change the world he lived in. He didn't want to be a victim but someone who chooses their future. The great lesson we learn from Mandela is that he was always highly self-aware of his emotions and thoughts. He also acknowledged his people's opinions and feelings and valued them more than anything else (Freiberg & Freiberg, 2018).

Oprah Winfrey

More recently, Oprah Winfrey can be considered an example of self-awareness and emotional intelligence. She came from nothing and managed to build a media empire, which is remarkable. You might believe the main reasons behind her success are her cognitive intelligence or talents, but that's not true. Oprah Winfrey owes her power and influence to her emotional intelligence. She not only acknowledges and expresses her emotions sincerely but also understands other people's feelings and thoughts and feels empathetic. She can be considered a lifelong learner who always aims to improve by challenging herself and exploring new opportunities. She also has solid relationships despite her success, as she's had the same life partner, best friend, and employees for decades (Richards, 2016). As you can see, she possesses all four components of emotional intelligence: Self-awareness, social awareness, self-management, and relationship management.

Warren Buffett

When he was a young businessman, Warren Buffet used to react with anger and resentment and struggled to control his behavior (Schwantes, 2022). In the heat of the moment, he could say words that he would have regretted the second after. He soon learned he had to improve his self-awareness skills and emotional intelligence if he wanted to become successful. Buffet's mentor, Tom Murphy, taught him how to become more self-aware through practicing a few simple rules. First, he had to do everything calmly. Screaming, yelling, or shouting was never going to be the right way to solve a problem and make his voice heard. Second, Tom Murphy taught him to wait for a day before criticizing or offending someone. According to him, there's always time to say negative things about someone so we can forget about them for a while. If we still want to say those words after some time, then we should say them. Otherwise, we'd better let it go and focus on more important issues. When Warren Buffet followed his mentor's advice and put it into practice, he started to become successful (Schwantes, 2022).

Indra Nooyi

Indra Nooyi has been PepsiCo's CEO for seven years and has managed to transform the company thanks to her emotional intelligence (White, 2020). Among the most important lessons she teaches us are the following. First, we must focus both on the short-term and long-term goals. Although short-term results can help us feel better and see concrete results, we mustn't undervalue or forget the big picture. Second, we must learn to take other perspectives into account, put ourselves in their shoes, and treat anyone with respect and understanding. Third, we must develop an open mind to be successful and make a difference in the world. We must promote dialog, cooperation, and exploration and adapt to change. Last but not least, Indra Nooyi teaches us to lead not only with our heads but also with our hearts. When she became CEO, one of the first things she did was send a letter to all the top executives' parents. She told them they should be proud of their children and highlighted their incredible effort and work inside the company. In turn, both parents and top executives felt appreciated and respected, thus feeling more connected to Indra Nooyi and PepsiCo (White, 2020).

EXERCISES AND ACTIVITIES FOR IMPROVING SELF-AWARENESS

In the section about techniques to enhance self-awareness, we looked at some general ways in which you can know yourself better. However, you can also try some practical and specific exercises to become more self-aware. Keep in mind you won't improve self-awareness if you only practice the following activities once. You must commit to putting effort into the exercises regularly and integrate them into your daily tasks. This way, you're more likely to improve your self-awareness rapidly and effectively. You'll find a list of exercises below. You can try all of them and choose the ones that you can better incorporate into your everyday activities.

- **Ask yourself self-awareness questions:** The best way to know yourself is by asking yourself questions you've never asked before or you've never considered carefully. Such questions help you become aware of the things you value in life, what goals you want to pursue, your personality, and how you relate to others. You can write down the answers in a journal and look at them from time to time. This way, you can modify them according to what you discover about yourself. Examples of questions are:

- Has your personality changed since childhood?
- Describe yourself in three words.
- What does your ideal "you" look like?
- What kinds of dreams and goals do you have and why are they important?
- Rank at least five of the most important things in your life and calculate the proportion of time you dedicate to each one.
- Is your personality similar to your parents'?
- What things scare you?
- What qualities do you admire the most in yourself?
- Are you satisfied with your relationships?
- Would you say you treat yourself better, at the same level, or worse than others?
- Describe your ideal romantic relationship or friendship.
- **Write morning pages:** A funny and interesting exercise you can practice every day is to write one or more pages as soon as you wake up. You don't have to pay attention to grammar, syntax, or repetitions— just go with the flow. Write down everything that crosses your mind, like a stream of consciousness. This exercise doesn't only help you declutter your mind but also become aware of your recurring thoughts and worries.
- **Name your emotions:** To become more self-aware, you must understand your feelings. Therefore, you must expand your vocabulary to identify the exact emotions you feel. When people ask you, "How are you?" you might tend to reply with a simple "Fine" or "Okay," but you can use a variety of words to label

your feelings. You can take a vocabulary and look for all the nouns you can find that refer to emotions or search on the internet. You'll find out you can be happy, sad, or angry in many ways and you can feel different intensities of the same emotion.

- **Create your life mission and vision:** Nowadays, big companies value elaborating on their mission and vision to make customers understand their purpose, their goals, and how they plan to achieve them. You can do the same for yourself: Write down your vision of the world, what you want to achieve, and how. This way, you'll understand your direction in life and priorities.

- **Write a regret letter:** A surprisingly cathartic exercise consists of writing a regret letter to your younger self, telling them what you wish you had known. You must record all the regrets you have and apologize for all the mistakes you made and the opportunities you missed over the years. Thanks to this activity, you accept your vulnerable and younger self and feel empowered to move on with your life with a positive attitude.

- **Record your ABCs:** This activity is extremely helpful after a stressful situation has occurred. It allows you to analyze the situation, how you perceive it, and what beliefs you have about adverse events in general. You have to write down your ABCs, which correspond to the Activating event that provokes a negative reaction in you, the Belief you've created after, and the Consequences of your new belief. You can't control the activating event but you can certainly control your beliefs and reactions. When you become aware of them, you can modify them to react more positively.

- **Write your eulogy:** It might sound creepy, but it helps you become aware of what you want to achieve in your life. When writing your eulogy, you must focus on how you want others to speak of you at your funeral, what they will remember about you, and which kind of people they will think you were. This way, you also understand what matters to you and how you imagine your best self. Writing about your death might be a daunting task, but it also reminds you that you won't live forever, thus urging you to find focus and clarity in your life.

- **Ask "Why" three times:** This exercise is as easy as it seems, as you just have to get to the roots of your decisions. Whenever you're about to make an important choice in your life, you must ask yourself "Why" three times. The question is very simple, so you might think you already analyzed the reasons behind your actions. However, you might struggle to find the origins of your choices. That's because asking yourself "Why" once is not enough to understand deep and specific issues.

In this chapter, we analyzed the concept of self-awareness and its significance in our everyday lives. We discovered it can have an incredible impact on our work environment and personal relationships and we can develop it by practicing some simple and useful techniques. We must build an open mind, identify our strengths and weaknesses, increase our focus, understand our emotional triggers, use our intuition, be self-disciplined, and apologize when it's needed. Then, we learned the amazing stories of some famous figures of our past and present history and how they used self-aware-ness and emotional intelligence to become successful and help people. Finally, we looked at more practical activities we can easily practice in our daily lives. Now that we've laid the foundation with self-awareness, we're ready to build upon it with effective communication skills. Are you ready to learn the art of active listening? Dive into the next chapter to find out how.

3

C-COMMUNICATION

 We have two ears and one mouth so that we can listen twice as much as we speak.

— EPICTETUS

When we communicate, especially during a conflict, we tend to forget that listening is more important than expressing our opinions. The ancient saying embodied in the above quote rings true today as it always has. We must listen more than we talk. However, not all forms of listening are equal: Depending on how we listen, we achieve different results. The most effective type of listening is active listening, which we'll discuss in this chapter. In the next sections, we'll discover the different types of listening, what active listening entails, how to apply it in various scenarios, and how to interpret and send nonverbal cues. The last section will show practical tips to enhance our listening skills. The reason why we'll focus on the role of active listening in communication is that it has many benefits in all aspects of our lives: It helps us develop deep and strong connections, boost leadership qualities, and advance in our careers (*Benefits of Active Listening*, 2021).

IMPORTANCE OF LISTENING IN COMMUNICATION

Communication is an integral part of our everyday life. We communicate and interact with other people constantly, sometimes without even noticing. In order to communicate your feelings and thoughts effectively, you must learn to express yourself and understand how, what, and when to talk. However, that's not the only element that constitutes effective communication. In fact, listening is just as important and goes beyond simply hearing what people tell you. There are seven types of listening: biased, discriminative, comprehensive, informational, empathetic, sympathetic, and critical (Perry, 2022b).

Biased listening is also known as selective listening because you only listen to what you want to hear. Consequently, you distort reality. For example, your superiors can congratulate you on a project you completed successfully and suggest improvements for the next one. If you practice biased listening, you only focus on the positive part of the conversation and forget about how you can do better next time. Discriminative listening is an innate type of listening that consists of focusing on various cues except words, like body language, tone of voice, posture, and so on. You use discriminative listening to understand the main context of a conversation.

For instance, you automatically use it while listening to a discussion in another language. As you can't understand what speakers are saying, you focus on other elements to identify the main topic and how they feel. Comprehensive listening is the opposite, as you concentrate on the words someone says to understand their message (Perry, 2022b).

Information listening helps you retain new concepts and learn. You mainly use it in educational or professional contexts when you have to acquire new knowledge or skills. Informational listening is more difficult than all the other types because you must be extremely concentrated and highly engaged. Empathetic listening allows you to put yourself in someone else's shoes and imagine how they feel and think. Sympathetic listening is similar but only involves understanding the speaker's emotions and providing support—it doesn't include taking their perspective. Finally, critical listening is connected with critical thinking and consists of analyzing a situation to find the best possible solution. You use critical thinking when you have to choose how to handle a difficult situation. For example, you use it to satisfy the requests of a particularly complicated client and look at the big picture (Perry, 2022b).

If you want to improve your communication skills and boost your relationships, you must do much more than understand the above types of listening: You must develop active listening. To grasp its meaning, you can consider its opposite, which is passive listening. When you practice passive listening, you don't carefully listen to what the speaker says but focus on something else. For example, your partner might tell you what they want to do during the weekend while you might think about your work or look at your smartphone. Conversely, active listening requires a conscious effort, attention, and empathy (Mulvania, 2020). It goes beyond merely hearing words and involves seeking to understand the meaning behind them. Active listening is a complex communication skill that implies listening to both verbal and nonverbal cues, paying attention to body language, being fully present, and being self-aware of the cues we use (Cuncic, 2022).

To understand how active listening applies to real life, let's look at an example. Imagine one of your colleagues complaining about another coworker. If you practice active listening, you show interest and ask them to tell you more about what happened. You let them talk and then tell them something like, "That must be tough! How does it make you feel?" This way, they keep expressing their emotions and thoughts. You ask other questions to clarify the situation and say something like, "I understand how you feel; maybe you need some time to think about what happened and what to do next." As you can see, you don't necessarily provide advice and you don't judge them for what they say or do. You simply listen and provide support with your words.

As you might guess, improving your active listening skills can have numerous positive effects on your personal and professional life. In fact, it allows you to take other people's perspective and understand their points of view, thus enhancing your relationships. Active listening is particularly helpful when you meet new people or find yourself in the middle of a conflict. When you pay attention to what others tell you and show interest, they feel comfortable and are more likely to keep talking to you and want to know more about you. During an argument, you can use your active listening skills to calm down the involved parties, listen to both, understand their points of view, and find a compromise that can satisfy both. Moreover, active listening is an essential skill you must develop to enhance your career opportunities and become an effective leader (Butler, 2021). A recent report has shown that employee misunderstanding makes British and American companies lose about $37 billion per year. In addition, the returns of businesses with poor communication practices are 53% lower than companies with effective communication practices (Butler, 2021). Active listening has a huge effect on the success and growth of businesses. That's why it's an essential skill for leaders, too.

PRINCIPLES OF ACTIVE LISTENING

The main principles that identify active listening are focus, comprehension, and feedback.

Focus

At this point, you might have understood you must pay attention to the speaker's words if you want to practice active listening. But do you know what it means? You might imagine yourself as a human recording machine and believe you must grasp every single word, nonverbal cue, and detail. However, this is impossible for everyone. When you focus on the quantity of words you listen to, you lose the opportunity to let what you hear sink, stop, and truly listen, make connections with others, process and understand, and see patterns during interactions. To maintain your focus on the conversation, you must eliminate all possible distractions, from your smartphone to noise around you and people who might interfere. For instance, you can meet your best friend for a coffee at a cafe that is not extremely crowded and you can turn your smartphone off or put it somewhere you won't see it or hear notifications. After you get rid of all distractions, you just have to sit and listen patiently. You don't need to grasp every single word and remember everything to practice active listening—you just need to be fully present with your mind and body.

Comprehension

When you practice active listening, you process the words you hear to understand, interpret, and speak when it's your turn. Comprehension is strictly connected with cognitive learning because you need to use your attention, memory, vocabulary, and grammar to understand what the speaker says and answer appropriately. The element of comprehension is essential before, during, and after a conversation. Before starting a discussion, you must consider who you'll be talking to and ask yourself why you want to listen. During the conversation, you create mental images and formulate hypotheses based on what the speaker says. After that, you assess if you correctly understood the speaker's message. Comprehension when practicing active listening is characterized by multiple skills. You must recognize literal meaning, which indicates you know at least something about the main topic and can understand the words you listen to. In addition, you recognize the vocabulary used and are able to infer the meaning of words from the main context and nonverbal cues. To develop comprehension, you also identify the main idea or heart of the matter and understand why the speaker chooses to discuss that particular topic or the main purpose of the conversation. Moreover, you can synthesize information, conclude from what you've heard, and understand the speaker's point of view and reasons. In other words, comprehension is the ability to analyze and correctly interpret the speaker's words.

Feedback

Feedback is a two-way communication process used to share information, suggestions, and opinions. Most people feel uncomfortable when receiving and giving feedback because they don't know how to do it properly. When we receive feedback, we tend to be defensive and feel like someone is attacking our personality and lifestyle. When we give feedback, we don't want to hurt the other person or be so polite that they don't understand our message. However, receiving and giving feedback is paramount to improving your relationships and becoming a better person. Active listening helps you control your verbal and nonverbal cues and pay attention to others' both when you receive and give feedback. You show appreciation and respect for the other person and focus both on their strengths and weaknesses without hurting their feelings. In addition, you encourage them to share their thoughts and emotions without making them feel judged. To give or receive feedback properly, you must prepare yourself. Think about why you want to engage in the conversation, what you plan to achieve, and what your main message will be. During the discussion, show empathy and respect, listen to the other person's perspective, and express your opinion clearly. When you want to give feedback to someone, remember it must be simple, specific, and actionable. Giving generic advice won't give the other person the tools to understand what they can do practically to improve. When you're about to receive feedback, accept you'll feel a bit uncomfortable in any case because someone will make considerations about your opinions and behaviors.

ACTIVE LISTENING ANYWHERE

You can practice active listening in all aspects of your life, from your professional to your personal life. Have you ever attended a long meeting or participated in a lengthy conversation and didn't know how to keep your focus? You might have tried your best to listen to what the speaker was saying and still, your mind might have wandered somewhere else. Practicing active listening helps you facilitate effective teamwork and fosters open communication with your coworkers. If you listen carefully to what they say, you show them you respect and value their opinions. Active listening is particularly helpful also during brainstorming sessions when you need to fully absorb other's ideas and find meaningful ways to add to the conversation.

To practice active listening in your workplace, you must limit distractions, as you learned in the previous section, and pay attention to your body language. Don't think about what you're going to say next or how you're going to introduce your new excellent idea; instead, concentrate on the person who's speaking to understand their words. To show you respect them, give them time to express their opinion by allowing moments of silence. Don't jump into the conversation as soon as they finish talking but wait for a few seconds to let them think and come up with other ideas. In addition, you can take notes to memorize what others say, show them you value their thoughts, and elaborate on the meaning of their words. You must maintain a positive learning attitude, especially during meetings and conferences, and find the perfect balance between letting others talk and sharing your experience.

Active listening is becoming an increasingly important skill also for leaders (Wooll, 2021). An authoritarian and judgmental leader might make employees feel afraid of them and of proposing their ideas, thus making them less likely to communicate effectively. In turn, a lack of communication can lead to poor productivity and team dysfunction. Active listening can improve your capacity as a leader because it teaches you to learn from anyone, even your employees. Stop believing you're always right just because you manage the company and start listening to everyone. Your employees who work every day certainly know better than you specific work dynamics and issues that you might not even notice from your office. Active listening also increases trust among team members because you show them you care about them. They feel appreciated and understood, so they're more likely to share their ideas and be honest. As you learned in the previous section, comprehension is an essential component of active listening. If you fail to comprehend a situation, you might propose ineffective solutions or not find the underlying problem. If you pay attention to what team members and employees tell you, you're more likely to understand the situation and find the most effective answers (Wooll, 2021).

Active listening allows you to better understand your business and provides insights into the day-to-day reality. If you show your employees you're there for them to listen to them and improve their work conditions, they'll feel more motivated and willing to maintain positive, open, and honest communication. In turn, you'll boost cooperation and innovation inside the company as your employees feel free to express their opinions. However, you might believe you'll never be able to improve your active listening skills because you're too busy. You might have to jump from one meeting to another, attend numerous calls, and have many thoughts inside your head. You can show your employees you care about them by taking notes of what they tell you and allocating some time to reflect on their words. Mark in your calendar a few minutes every day when you focus on what your employees and team members told you. Analyze their words and think about ways in which you can avoid conflict, resolve an issue, or improve their work conditions. If you're willing to dedicate time to reflect on what your employees tell you, then you'll certainly improve your active listening skills.

NONVERBAL COMMUNICATION IN ACTIVE LISTENING

To communicate effectively and practice active listening, you must become aware of how nonverbal communication works. Research has found that 80% of communication occurs through nonverbal cues, while only 20% focuses on words (Cherry, 2023a). This means you must pay much more attention to what people express with their bodies than with their words. There are nine types of nonverbal communication characterized by different levels of consciousness. In some cases, we can be perfectly aware of the nonverbal cues we're sending, while in others, we struggle to control our body reactions and to make people understand our true intentions and feelings (Cherry, 2023a).

The first thing we notice when talking to someone is their facial expression, which is responsible for the majority of nonverbal communication (Cherry, 2023a). Research has discovered that nonverbal communication can vary among cultures, while some facial expressions are universal and can be identified by anyone around the world. If a person smiles, we automatically assume they're happy. Body language is a more subtle type of nonverbal communication, as researchers are still looking for conclusive evidence on how it works. For instance, crossed arms generally indicate a defensive posture, thus representing closure and protection. Conversely, hands on the hips imply aggressiveness and control. Body language and posture can illustrate some feelings and attitudes but they shouldn't be overly interpreted. In fact, a person can cross their arms for various reasons and not only because they feel attacked and need to defend themselves. If you want, you can increase your knowledge about body language, but bear in mind that it's not an exact science and can mislead you when interpreting others' emotions and thoughts (Cherry, 2023a).

A type of nonverbal communication that you can easily control is gestures, like pointing your finger, waving your hand, or giving a "thumbs up" (Cherry, 2023a). While facial expressions are universal, gestures are extremely dependent on culture. For example, creating the shape of a "V" with your index and middle finger symbolizes "victory" in the US and other countries, while it might be considered an insult in Australia. Another important type of nonverbal communication is proxemics, which is often called personal space. Some people might enjoy staying close, while others might prefer maintaining more distance between themselves and other people. In general, people maintain a distance between 18 inches and 4 feet when having a casual conversation with a person they don't know. Paralinguistics involves vocal communication but it's different from the simple words and language used. In fact, it refers to the pitch, tone of voice, inflection, loudness, and similar elements. If someone uses a high tone of voice, they might be angry, while if they use a high-pitched tone, it might mean they're excited or surprised (Cherry, 2023a).

A fascinating type of nonverbal communication is eye gaze. By looking into someone's eyes, you can understand many things, like if they're interested and attracted or hostile (Cherry, 2023a). When you like someone or something, your pupils dilate and start blinking more. In general, steady eye contact is perceived as trustworthy and sincere, while shifty eyes might indicate avoidance or lies. However, research hasn't found any conclusive evidence about eye gaze accurately predicting lying behavior. Surprisingly, objects and images are also considered a type of nonverbal communication, as they can convey clear messages. The way we decorate our houses, what items we wear, or what avatar we choose to represent us online can send specific information. Our appearance, like our clothes or hairstyle, is also used to communicate with the people around us. Last but not least, haptics or touch is another type of nonverbal communication. A gentle touch can signal care, concern, and love, while a decisive and firm touch might express power and control. You can use the different types of nonverbal communication to express your thoughts and feelings more clearly and efficiently. Just keep in mind some factors might change from one culture to another and some types might convey ambiguous messages.

TIPS AND EXERCISES FOR ENHANCING LISTENING ABILITIES

To improve your active listening skills, remember some easy tips when talking to someone else. You can write them down on a piece of paper or note them on your smartphone and always bring them with you. This way, you can practice the tips wherever you go and look at them before starting a conversation. Try to use them as much as you can.

- **Listen before speaking:** This tip might seem obvious, but we often forget to let others talk before expressing our opinions. If you want to avoid misunderstandings and answer appropriately, you must listen first. You might feel the urge to say something that you consider useful or relevant, but you have to fight that temptation. Just wait until the other person finishes talking. After all, we all want to be listened to and that's probably what you'll want others to do with you.

- **Maintain eye contact:** If you want to avoid distractions and make the speaker understand you're carefully listening to them, you must look at them. They might avoid your gaze if they discuss a sensitive topic or are shy, but this doesn't mean you should stop looking at them. The main problem with eye contact is that you have to do it properly. If you stare too much, you might intimidate or make the speaker feel uncomfortable. If you look away, they might think you're not interested in the conversation. Therefore, you must keep practicing and looking at others' reactions to the way you maintain eye contact. If you notice they feel comfortable, then that's how you should look at them.

- **Focus on nonverbal cues:** As you already learned, nonverbal cues might be even more important than verbal ones, so pay attention to them. In addition to listening to the speaker's words, you must look at their body. At the same time, you can reflect on the nonverbal cues you send to them and how you can use them to convey your message more efficiently.

- **Visualize the speaker's words:** A good way of understanding and remembering what the speaker says is to visualize their words. You can create a mental image and relate the topic they discuss to something you're familiar with. If they tell you how their day went and what they did, you can try to imagine them doing all the things they say. If they talk about their Saturday night and how they enjoyed the new restaurant they tried, you can think about the dishes they ate and how they tasted.

- **Avoid judgment:** In most cases, people talk because they feel the need to vent or express their thoughts and feelings. Therefore, they don't need you to tell them how they should think and feel or judge them in any way. You must use neutral language and let them express their opinion as much as they feel like it. You might find a situation unacceptable as the speaker starts describing it and then you think it might make sense as they keep talking. You must know the entire story before expressing your opinion and giving advice if the speaker wants you to help them.

- **Ask questions:** To have a clear idea of what the speaker means, you can ask clarifying questions. For instance, repeat a sentence with your words and ask them if you understood correctly what they said. To show you're interested in the conversation, you can also replace closed-ended with open-ended questions. Instead of asking them something like, "Are you happy?" tell them, "How does this situation make you feel?" This way, they're more likely to deepen their thoughts and clarify their emotions. Remember to be patient and wait to ask questions. For example, you can take the occasion when a natural pause or break occurs. Otherwise, you must let the speaker talk.

- **Provide feedback:** If you want the speaker to understand you're truly listening to them, you must show them your engagement while they talk. Maintaining eye contact is not enough because it only indicates you're looking at them—but are you truly listening or thinking about something else? You can use verbal and nonverbal feedback to make the speaker understand you're following the conversation. Nod your head, lean forward, and change facial expressions according to what they say, or you can use phrases like, "I understand," "Right," or "I see." This way, you don't interrupt the speaker while manifesting your engagement.

You can practice the above tips in all sorts of contexts, from your workplace to your house. If you think about it, you have plenty of opportunities to become a better listener, so take advantage of them to improve. The more you practice, the more you'll master this skill.

In this chapter, we discussed the essential element of effective communication: active listening. We discovered there are various types of listening, but active listening is the communication skill we must develop to become happier and more successful. Next, we learned the main components of active listening: Comprehension, focus, and feedback. We also looked at ways in which active listening applies to work-places and how useful it is for effective leaders. Then, we learned about the different types of nonverbal communication and how we must use them carefully. Finally, we discussed some tips to practice and improve our active listening skills. However, active listening is just one piece of the puzzle. Being able to understand the feelings behind the words is another big part. That's why the next chapter will focus on empathy, which is as important as active listening to mastering emotional intelligence.

4

U-UNDERSTANDING

> *You never really understand a person until you consider things from his point of view...until you climb into his skin and walk around in it.*

— HARPER LEE

Self-awareness and active listening are essential elements of emotional intelligence that can help you improve your mental and physical health and increase your performance and success at work. However, there's another feature that can boost your relationships in your professional and personal life: empathy. If you don't empathize with the people around you, they'll feel like you can't understand them and put yourself in their shoes. That's why you must become more empathetic to make the right decisions in your life. In this chapter, you'll learn the role of empathy in emotional intelligence and leadership and how it can improve your personal relationships. Finally, you'll find a list of hands-on exercises that you can practice to develop your empathy skills.

THE ESSENCE OF EMPATHY IN EI

Empathy is the ability to emotionally understand what other people are going through (Cherry, 2023b). If you're empathetic, you're able to put yourself in others' shoes and see things from their point of view. If you notice someone grieving because they lost a loved one, you can immediately imagine yourself in the same situation and reflect on how you would feel. Being self-aware and understanding your emotions doesn't automatically lead to identifying others' feelings. You can be well-attuned to your inner self and still struggle to understand how others might feel. If you're empathetic, you're a good listener and people feel comfortable discussing their problems with you. You easily grasp how they feel and spend a lot of time reflecting on others' emotions. You care deeply for others and try to help everyone who's suffering. Empathy is a skill that can have many benefits on your personal and professional relationships, like helping you build stronger and deeper connections, promoting helping behaviors, and managing your emotions effectively. However, it might also have negative effects. In fact, you might feel drained by social situations because you try to understand everyone's true feelings, you might feel overwhelmed by tragic events in your life or around the world, and you might struggle to set boundaries in your relationships (Cherry, 2023b).

When talking about empathy, people tend to confuse it with two similar concepts: sympathy and compassion. Although they're linked with each other, they have different meanings. If you're empathetic, you feel how others feel. If you're sympathetic, you simply feel sorry and bad for them (Perry, 2022a). You don't put yourself in their shoes but judge them by perceiving their situation from your specific point of view. In other words, sympathy corresponds to a superficial level of understanding of others' emotions, while empathy is deeper. This last concept is also slightly different from compassion. If you feel compassionate, you not only feel how others feel but are also willing to do something about it. Therefore, you feel the urge to help other people to make them feel better. We could say compassion is the next level or step of empathy. If you're empathetic, you put yourself in others' shoes, but you don't necessarily want to do something to help them (Perry, 2022a).

Empathy is characterized by two components: emotional and cognitive response (*The Psychology of Emotional and Cognitive Empathy*, n.d.). An emotional response occurs when you understand others' emotions. You feel how they feel, you also feel distressed to hear about their problems and difficulties, and you want to do something for them. This last aspect corresponds with the concept of compassion when you feel the urge to help those who suffer. A cognitive response happens when you can assess others' mental states and what they might think about their specific situation (*The Psychology of Emotional and Cognitive Empathy*, n.d.).

Researchers have tried to understand the reasons behind being empathetic but they haven't found a clear answer yet

(*The Psychology of Emotional and Cognitive Empathy*, n.d.). We might empathize because we feel altruistic and want to help others or we believe we might get some sort of advantage from being empathetic. Researchers have also identified two theories to explain how we empathize. The Simulation Theory claims that we empathize because we simulate or represent the same emotion we perceive in someone else to understand how they feel. This theory is supported by the scientific discovery of mirror neurons, specific neurons we all have that allow us to reproduce someone else's actions and emotions. The Theory of Mind states that we empathize thanks to our ability to understand how someone feels and thinks based on rules of how we should think and feel. Over the years, we have developed our theories about how someone should behave according to their mental state. Then, we put them into practice by observing others and making predictions or trying to explain why they behave in a certain way. If someone feels happy, we can predict they will smile, laugh, and show enthusiasm. If a person feels sad, they're likely to close themself off, avoid social contact, and feel down. That's what the Theory of Mind is about (*The Psychology of Emotional and Cognitive Empathy*, n.d.).

Empathy might be a complex concept to understand and is involved in so many social interactions that you might need some real-life examples to grasp its meaning. It manifests in all situations in which you manage to feel as others feel. For example, you're empathetic if you feel the same emotions your friend is feeling while they tell you about an incredible event that occurred to them. If they feel excited, you feel excited, too. Alternatively, they might tell you a moving story and you might feel the need to cry. When talking to someone, you might realize they misunderstood your words and realize the reasons why. If you feel guilty, then you're being empathetic. In fact, empathy is not as straightforward as you might think. If you feel empathetic, it doesn't mean you automatically feel the same emotion others feel. You might also adapt it and express another emotion that can be associated with it.

EMPATHY'S ROLE IN LEADERSHIP

Empathy is an extremely useful skill for leaders, as it can enhance positive emotions and experiences in the workplace (Brower, 2021). Recently, a study conducted on more than 800 employees achieved incredible results. Participants were divided between those who had an empathetic leader and those who had a leader with low levels of empathy. Sixty-one percent of employees with an empathetic leader reported feeling more innovative in their workplace compared to only 13% of the other group of participants. Seventy-six percent also claimed to feel more engaged during their daily tasks, while only 32% of those with a less empathetic leader did. Female workers who felt valued and appreciated were more likely to retain their jobs and keep working for the same company than those who didn't have an empathetic leader. In addition, employees with an empathetic leader were more likely to consider their workplace inclusive and they had a better work-life balance because their leaders understood their personal needs were as important as their professional ones. Another study analyzed the effects of empathy in the decision-making process and found that it increased cooperation among team members and fostered more empathy inside the company (Brower, 2021).

If you want to become an effective leader, you can also accompany your words with your actions, thus transforming your empathy into compassion. Do something nice for your employees, even if it won't give you any evident benefit in the short or long term. This way, they'll know you care about them and appreciate them. You don't need to raise their salaries or give them gifts before the Christmas holidays— just provide support to improve their everyday experience at work.

If you want, you can become an empathetic leader, which means you have a genuine interest in what your employees or team members think and feel, how they face daily challenges, and what goals they want to achieve (Roncero, 2021). As an empathetic leader, you make a concrete effort to understand and know more about your employees' lives and you make them feel safe and cared for, thus developing a strong relationship based on mutual trust. If you think empathy is not an essential skill for leaders, reflect on two possible scenarios. Imagine a workplace where employees feel insecure and obey all your orders, but feel stressed out and prefer looking out for themselves rather than valuing the team or company as a whole. Now, imagine another workplace where employees feel secure and look forward to going to. The atmosphere is relaxed and everyone manages to be productive and happy at the same time. Employees know they can rely on each other, so they give more importance to the company as a whole than themselves. You'll probably choose to work in the second type of workplace, where empathy unites everyone. The more relaxed and appreciated your employees feel, the more productive and successful your company will be. Your employees don't work for you—you work for them.

What distinguishes an empathetic leader from other styles of leadership? You motivate your employees and team members to do the best they can and be the best version of themselves to achieve excellent results inside the company. You know every opinion counts and all your employees feel appreciated. You also foster open, honest, and constant communication among all your team members. To keep updated with what happens in their professional and personal lives, you often interact with them and ask them about how they feel and what they think. In addition, you make them feel supported because you try your best to help them when they need you. They know you'll always have their back and be there for them. Last but not least, being an empathetic leader involves creating a sense of community, purpose, and belonging inside the company. All employees feel connected and work toward the same goals.

To become an empathetic leader, you must be approachable, which means that your employees and team members see you as a human being and not a robot or a king who tells them what to do and nothing more. They perceive you as a guide or someone they can go to if they need help. Literally and metaphorically, you always have the door of your office open. Your employees and team members don't feel inferior to you but at the same level because you let them express their opinions and treat them with respect. As an empathetic leader, you must also involve everyone in the conversations and appreciate every idea. You let anyone inside the team or company talk, share their thoughts, brainstorm together, and give feedback to overcome challenges most effectively. Consequently, an empathetic leader is also flexible because they're ready to change their opinion if one of their employees or team members suggests a solution better than theirs. Ultimately, an empathetic leader empowers everyone in the company.

Research has proven that empathy has a genetic basis (Roncero, 2021). Therefore, some people are naturally more empathetic than others. However, empathy is not only a trait but also a skill because everyone can improve. Like a muscle, empathy can be trained if you pay attention to your employees' needs and wants and show them you care about them. If you set the example first, your team members are more likely to follow you and foster the development of a positive and relaxed work environment.

EMPATHY IN PERSONAL RELATIONSHIPS

Empathy is also crucial to building healthy and strong relationships outside your workplace. If you're empathetic, you can understand your partner and loved ones on a deeper level, thus making them feel cherished and appreciated for who they are. Consequently, you increase the quality and satisfaction of your relationships. Empathy allows you to understand what they need and want, what makes them happy, and what can hurt them. Instead of simply reacting to their requests, being empathetic provides the tools to respond in a way that meets their needs. Interestingly, research has found that couples who feel more emotionally connected are the ones who express higher levels of empathy toward each other (Rickardsson, n.d.). The more you show you feel empathetic toward your partner and friends, the more you'll deepen your relationships. In addition, you'll reduce unnecessary and prolonged conflicts. If you're empathetic, you can understand your loved ones' points of view and try to find a compromise that can be beneficial for both of you. This way, you decrease the probability of escalation and show others you care about their feelings and thoughts.

Research has also discovered that one of the key elements for a happy and long relationship is empathy (Rickardsson, n.d.). When you're empathetic, you show your significant other you dedicate time and effort to the relationship and to putting yourself into their shoes. Moreover, you enhance resilience in the couple, thus making both you and your partner more equipped to handle challenges and tough times. That's because you're better at understanding what each other needs during difficult periods and can communicate effectively. Partners who are empathetic toward each other tend to work together as a team to overcome obstacles instead of letting tough times tear them apart. Empathy is an essential skill you can use to improve your relationship during both good and bad times.

How can you understand if you or your loved ones lack empathy? They might tend to appear overly critical and impatient, thus making others believe they walk on eggshells. They might make other people feel unheard and misunderstood and look insensitive. For example, they might answer, "Get over it," when someone is in distress and is facing a difficult situation. If you or one of your loved ones lack empathy, you can see it from the feedback you usually give. You might tell your best friend they don't earn enough money because they don't work hard enough or they've been burglarized because they haven't been careful. You might believe people around you are too sensitive because they appear to get easily offended by your jokes or don't feel supported when you try to help them. That's normal for people who aren't empathetic because they don't understand how their words and actions could hurt others.

If you realize you lack empathy, you can improve. Keep in mind nobody is fully empathetic or doesn't possess this skill at all, as we're all in the middle of a spectrum (Reid, 2023). You don't lack empathy but might have low levels. If that's the case, you can develop your empathic skills. Practice the activities discussed in the previous chapters or try different ones, like working on your vulnerability. If you have low levels of empathy, you might hide behind indifference to avoid showing your true emotions and thoughts. You might have been taught that vulnerability is a weakness and you mustn't show your flaws. However, that's exactly what makes you unique and appreciated by others. If you show your vulnerabilities to your significant other and loved ones, you'll deepen your relationships and open the doors to empathetic interactions. You mustn't be ashamed of your negative feelings and thoughts, as we all have them and have to deal with them in some way. Open up to your loved ones and let them help you face difficulties together.

Another tip you can follow to become more empathetic is to clearly express your needs. Don't be afraid to tell your loved ones what you want from them and what can make you feel better. If you're not used to expressing your needs, you can start with simple requests, like asking your partner to accompany you for a walk to de-stress. Once you've become comfortable with simple requests, you can work your way up to clearly explaining your fundamental emotional needs. One reason why you might feel less empathetic toward your significant other and loved ones is resentment. If you've never expressed your needs and wants properly in your relationships, you might still hold a grudge or feel hurt by events that occurred months or even years before. You might convince yourself you managed to successfully overcome a difficult moment and move on while you still carry some pain with you. If you don't get rid of that pain, you might blame your partner or loved ones for your negative emotions and feel less empathetic toward them. Try to get to the root causes of lacking empathy and solve them together with your significant other. Alternatively, you might have low levels of empathy because you don't receive enough of it from others. In this case, don't be afraid to be the one who boosts the relationship. Show empathy to encourage your loved ones to do the same. It might require time and effort and you might not see results immediately. After some time, you'll gradually notice a change in the people around you.

ACTIVITIES TO DEVELOP EMPATHETIC SKILLS

You can improve your empathetic skills by practicing some simple and quick exercises every day. You don't have to revolutionize your life to develop empathy—you'll just need to do little things. Below, you'll find a list of activities you can try.

- **Read:** A funny and relaxing way of improving your empathetic skills is through reading. Fantasy novels and books that analyze characters' emotions can teach you a lot about how to be more empathetic and understand others' feelings. High-quality fiction books can be so precise that they provide details of facial expressions, physical reactions, and internal thoughts, thus giving you all the tools to understand others' emotions and ideas. You don't have to read a whole book in a week, as you can just read a few pages every day. If you focus on reading high-quality books, you'll rapidly gain many insights into the human mind. If you don't feel comfortable reading long books, you can start with shorter ones.
- **Do something nice for someone:** Showing others you love them and care about them can improve your empathetic skills, as you also become aware of their physical and emotional reactions to your gestures. Try to do something nice for someone you love or even someone you don't know, and see how they react. For instance, you can open the door to your coworker who's arrived a bit late or leave a kind and loving note to your partner. If you want,

you can combine active listening and empathy by dedicating a few minutes of your time to listening to your significant other. You don't necessarily have to use money to make someone happy—your time and energy are enough. You might feel stressed and too busy to make even small gestures, but you must give it a try because it will provide incredible benefits to your mental and physical health, even if you feel completely drained.

- **Be kinder to yourself:** Think about a situation you're struggling with or a mistake you've recently made. Then, ask yourself how you feel and reflect on what you keep repeating to yourself. Are you used to saying you're incompetent, you don't deserve to be happy, you'll never make it, and similar sentences? If so, you can change your life by developing empathy and being kinder to yourself. Whenever you catch yourself criticizing harshly your work, life, and goals, ask yourself what you would say to your best friend if they were in the same situation. You'll probably find out you would tell them exactly the opposite. You would make them feel better by telling them something like, "Don't give up," "I know you can make it," "You're very good at your job," and similar things. Stop being harsh on yourself and accept you make mistakes and struggle as anyone else. If the people you love deserve to feel better and be encouraged, then you deserve it, too.

- **Disagree without debating:** To practice this exercise, you have to have a conversation with someone you disagree with, like a neighbor or colleague who shares different opinions about specific topics. When a contentious issue arises, show them you disagree with them and express your personal opinion. At this point, the other person might get upset or nervous, and you might feel like you're about to have a heated argument. To avoid escalation, show empathy by explaining how you came to your opinion. Show them you're willing to have a healthy conversation with them and share a small part of yourself and your ideas. Then, ask them to do the same. This way, you both feel free to express your thoughts and try to understand the other's point of view, thus increasing the probability of feeling empathetic toward each other. This exercise might be a bit uncomfortable in the beginning, but it can help you improve your relationships.

- **Praise empathic behavior:** When someone achieves an important goal, we're used to celebrating and congratulating them for their results. We should learn to do the same when we notice empathic behavior. If your significant other tries to understand your point of view and puts themselves in your shoes, you must praise their effort and show them you appreciate what they're doing for you. You can do the same at work when someone calmly expresses their opinion without judging or feeling superior to their colleagues. If you encourage empathy in others, they're more likely to show it more often and be more empathetic toward you.

- **Be curious:** The most effective way of developing empathy is by being curious and challenging yourself with new experiences. If you often try something new, you become more aware of your feelings and thoughts and express them effectively. Get out of your comfort zone and develop new skills. Trying new activities makes you humble because you're not an expert and must learn from the beginning. In turn, humility makes you feel more empathetic. To boost your curiosity, ask questions to the people around you and try to learn from them. For instance, you can talk to a new, inexperienced colleague to discover if they can teach you something you don't know. By being curious and challenging yourself, you'll not only develop empathy but also enrich your life.

In this chapter, we understood what empathy is and why it's vital to develop our relationships and decision-making skills. Thanks to this skill, we can put ourselves in others' shoes, understand their points of view, and improve our work environment and personal relationships. Employees of empathetic leaders report feeling more satisfied, innovative, and appreciated. To become an empathetic leader, you must show your employees and team members you care about their feelings, thoughts, and work conditions, and you'll always do your best to make them feel happier. To improve your relationships, you must show your vulnerabilities and let go of past hurts. Finally, we looked at some useful and easy activities we can try to enhance our empathetic skills, like reading fiction books or being kind to others and ourselves. However, developing emotional intelligence involves more than just understanding others. We must also learn to control our impulsive reactions and take a pause before acting. The next chapter will provide invaluable insights into why and how to pause before responding to different situations.

HEY FRIENDS!

We're on a mission! Did you know that understanding your emotions can be like having a superpower? It's true! And "The Secret of Emotional Intelligence" is like your personal guide to unlocking this power. This book isn't just for grown-ups; it's for anyone who wants to be happier, make better choices, and get along better with others – that includes you!

Our Big Goal

We want to share the secrets of emotional intelligence with everyone! It's like sharing a map to treasure, but the treasure is a happier and more understanding you. Our dream is to help as many people as possible learn these secrets.

Your Role in Our Adventure

You can be a hero in our story! How? By sharing what you think about the book. When you tell others how "The Secret of Emotional Intelligence" helped you, you're helping them too. It's like passing on a magic key that can open doors to better friendships, less stress, and more smiles.

Leaving a review is super easy! It won't cost you a penny, and it'll take just a minute. But your words could be the nudge someone else needs to pick up this book and start their journey to understanding emotions better. Your review could be the reason someone else becomes happier and more confident.

Ready to Help?

All you need to do is share what you liked about the book, what you learned, and how it made you feel. Your honest thoughts are like a helping hand to someone else who is looking for a way to understand their emotions better. Just scan the QR code to leave your review!

Thank You!

By helping us, you're making a big difference. You're not just reviewing a book; you're spreading kindness and understanding. And that's a pretty awesome thing to do.

5

S-SLOW DOWN

> *Between stimulus and response, there is a space. In that space is our power to choose our response.*
>
> — VIKTOR E. FRANKL

It takes just a fraction of a moment to react impulsively. But it's in that short time frame that we have the power to fight immediate reactions. If you've ever responded without thinking, you might know learning to pause can make a world of difference in your personal and professional life. In this chapter, you'll learn everything you need about impulsive reactions and how to overcome them. First, you'll discover the short and long-term effects of instinctive reactions and how pausing can transform your interactions and decisions. Next, you'll find out the mental processes behind taking a pause and real-life examples of pausing before acting. Finally, you'll find practical techniques to slow down.

THE DRAWBACKS OF IMPULSIVE REACTIONS

Impulsive behavior is defined as inappropriate actions that don't consider the risks and consequences (Salters-Pedneault, 2023). Impulsivity is usually associated with undesirable outcomes because the person who engages in impetuous behavior doesn't think carefully about what they want to do. Impulsivity is also a sign of a mental health disorder, like bipolar disorder, borderline personality disorder, and attention deficit hyperactivity disorder. However, displaying instinctive behavior doesn't automatically mean suffering from the above mental issues. If you often engage in impulsive behavior, you might easily get into trouble by causing arguments or making bad decisions, thus undermining your relationships and your mental and physical health. Impulsive people might also have financial or legal issues because of their inability to manage their income and interactions effectively. If you engage in impetuous behavior, people might define you as hot-headed, unstable, and unpredictable. Therefore, they might struggle to be there for you and understand what you want and need (Salters-Pedneault, 2023).

Abrupt behaviors are considered inappropriate in terms of potential risk and scale. If you're used to buying impulsively, you might easily lose all your money and be broke or have huge debts to repay. In addition, you might react excessively to apparently harmless events. For example, you might feel extremely satisfied with your relationship with your partner and show them how much you love them one day, but then, they do something you don't understand or like, and you feel depressed and disappointed the day after. If you often engage in impulsive behaviors, you're likely to manifest unstable emotions that people around you struggle to comprehend. Sometimes, people confuse impulsivity with compulsion, which are two different concepts. If you have a compulsion, you're aware your behavior is considered unusual by the majority of people but you can't stop doing it. If you're impulsive, you might not realize the effects of your actions and not consider them unhealthy or uncommon. Examples of instinctive behaviors include changing plans from one moment to another, tending to start anew every now and then, feeling offended by people who criticize you, having emotional outbursts, oversharing, and escalating arguments. In general, you often change ideas and want to try different things. You might join and quit groups from one day to another or often leave your jobs to find something different (Salters-Pedneault, 2023).

Some people are more predisposed to impulsive behavior than others due to some risk factors (Salters-Pedneault, 2023). Younger people are more likely to engage in hasty behavior because their brains are still developing and boys and men are more predisposed than girls and women. Drugs and alcohol can also contribute to the manifestation of impulsivity. If you suffer from a trauma, like abuse or violence, you're also more likely to engage in impulsive behavior. Finally, family history also plays a role: If one of your relatives manifested such behavior or suffered from a mental health disorder linked with it, you're likely to develop the same disease. You might wonder what exactly causes you to react instinctively. Researchers are trying to answer that question but they haven't found any concrete evidence yet. However, some environmental and genetic factors can provoke impulsive behaviors (Salters-Pedneault, 2023).

Your childhood and the way your parents raised you play a fundamental role in developing impetuous reactions (Salters-Pedneault, 2023). If your parents didn't help you manage your emotions and thoughts, you might have struggled to regulate yourself on your own. You might have developed unhealthy behavior that nobody ever corrected, thus transforming it into habits. However, having a difficult childhood doesn't imply engaging in impulsive behavior. In fact, the environment plays an important role, too. If you grow up in a place where teachers, friends, and the people around you support you and help you regulate your emotions, you can fight impulsive behaviors effectively. Genetic factors that influence your probability of engaging in such actions include mutation that impacts the production of the neurotransmitters dopamine and serotonin, which are responsible for your mood and cognition (Salters-Pedneault, 2023).

Impulsivity can have both short and long-term negative effects on your success. In the short term, it might hinder your relationships with your colleagues and loved ones because they might feel attacked or confused by your words and actions. If you tend to react instinctively, you might express an opinion one day and do the exact opposite the day after, thus making others doubt your personality and honesty. In the long term, they might decide to end their relationship with you. If you have a partner, you might risk losing them because you make impulsive expenses, thus spending a lot of money, or because you tend to change ideas about what you want to do in your future. In general, people might easily misinterpret your actions and not understand why you change so easily. As we usually look for stability, we tend to avoid those who appear unstable. However, you mustn't blame yourself if you often engage in impulsive behaviors. It's important to face all obstacles, learn to take a pause, and try to control your reactions.

If you feel ashamed and believe you're the only one, you must know everyone can be impetuous, even the most famous and important people. World history is full of impulsive decisions that lead to disaster in one way or another (Dreher & Nowak, 2019). The renowned Queen of France, Marie Antoinette, made a last-minute decision that cost her her life. French rebels were devastating Paris and Marie Antoinette and her husband decided to flee. The General advised them to take two simple carriages to leave the capital, but she insisted they had to travel together on a fancier transport. While leaving, some armed villagers recognized the carriage and attacked them. Their capture was instrumental in their subsequent execution. Another fascinating story about bad last-minute decisions involves the famous Titanic. Right before departure, the cruise company decided to replace the ship's second officer in a rush, who forgot to give a pair of keys to his substitute. Those keys opened a locker where there were the binoculars needed to spot large obstacles, like icebergs. As you might guess, the new ship's second officer would have truly needed the keys to get the binoculars. Why the company cruise made this last-minute change is still a mystery (Dreher & Nowak, 2019).

THE POWER OF PAUSING AND THOUGHTFUL RESPONDING

To fight the urge to react impulsively to events, you must learn how to pause. You might consider the previous statement obvious and not helpful, as you might have already understood you should pause before reacting. However, do you know what pausing deeply means? Think about a typical day in your life and focus on all the people, things, and noise that surround you. You might wake up and look at your smartphone to check notifications on your social media. Next, you might answer your colleagues or make an important phone call for your job while having breakfast. You might live in a crowded city where you often hear horns, sirens, or people yelling at each other. When you're with your colleagues or friends, you might focus on talking and interacting. When you're alone, you might take advantage of that time to watch your favorite TV series or chat on your smartphone.

The one activity you might struggle to accomplish is enjoying silence. We're all so busy multitasking and pursuing our goals that we often forget the importance of taking a pause and focusing on our inner selves. Most times, we also fear silence and prefer avoiding it at all costs because it makes us feel empty and uncomfortable. Conversely, pausing can have incredible effects on our mental and physical health. Research has found that relaxation promotes balance and renewal (Bradley, 2018). Taking a break from noise and staying quiet and still for a few minutes every day can already re-energize you and make you feel more relaxed.

In addition, pausing can increase your creativity and make you more concentrated and productive (Blaschka, 2022). Has someone ever told you creativity increases when you do nothing and just rest? That's actually true. Research confirms daydreaming helps us come up with innovative ideas and improves our problem-solving skills. Without taking regular breaks from all the chaos around you, you might suffer from anxiety, stress, or burnout, thus weakening your mental and physical health. You risk aging faster and becoming more susceptible to viruses and infections. Learning to block some time on your calendar just for yourself allows you to keep your focus on the things that truly matter in life. If you feel overwhelmed by all your responsibilities and duties, you might believe everything is urgent and important, which is not true. You don't have to do everything—only the things that are right for you. Finally, being constantly busy doesn't make you more productive, while downtime can. Your career and personal life will progress only if you allow yourself to take a pause (Blaschka, 2022).

If you're a leader, taking a pause is essential to protect and improve your business and make your employees and team members feel valued. Many executives and managers end up micromanaging their business and being short-term oriented even if they would like to never forget the big picture and think strategically. The main reason why many leaders fall into the trap of focusing on short-term problems and goals is that they're not used to taking a break to listen to their inner selves and shut down all noise and chaos. They keep controlling their business and tackling all issues as they occur without reflecting on the long-term benefits. They enter the spiral of facing all obstacles as soon as they appear without considering various options. At some point, they become overwhelmed by all problems and can't distinguish between what's important and what can wait. If you recognize yourself in the above description, you can learn to take a pause to analyze all the pros and cons of tackling each issue and what the best course of action is.

How can you learn to pause? If you're not used to integrating breaks into your daily life, you might struggle to find the time for them. Therefore, you must make them as short and easy as possible. Decide a few moments during the day in which you would have time and the right attitude to take a pause. For instance, you can take a few moments for yourself before getting out of bed. Some people might turn their alarm off and rush because they're afraid of being late already. Instead, try staying in bed for a few more seconds or minutes. Don't think about what you have to do next and all your responsibilities but check on your mental health. Did you sleep well? How do you feel? Then, focus on the air you breathe in and out. If you notice your breathing is rapid, slow it down. When you're ready to get out of bed, think about a thing that might make your day worthwhile and commit to accomplishing it. A nice, little gesture can be enough.

Potentially, you can take a pause from all the chaos inside and outside your head whenever you want to. For example, try taking a shower without running your day's agenda. Focus on the physical sensations the water produces on your body and how it makes you feel. If you don't manage to keep your focus, try singing your favorite songs, which is certainly better than worrying about your duties. In addition, you can take a break while drinking and eating. Try savoring the first sip of coffee in the morning by sitting on a chair and switching off your mind for a few minutes. During your lunch break, go to a calm place where nobody will disturb you and focus on your meal. Analyze the physical and emotional sensations it produces and if you truly like what you're eating. At the end of your working day, take a few moments to relax or play. If you have kids, you can dedicate some time to them and just have fun. Alternatively, take a walk around your neighborhood, read a book, or keep a journal. When you're ready to go to sleep, take a few moments to reflect on what happened during the day, concentrating on the positive events. What worked well for you today? Did someone or something make you feel happier? Why? Focusing on the good things that happened to you before going to bed can help you fall asleep faster and sleep better. To integrate pauses into your daily life, think about all the activities you do and how you can take advantage of them to slow down.

PAUSING AND DECISION-MAKING

Pausing before an important decision is paramount to evaluate the situation carefully. Some people tend to believe their first reaction is the best they can have and base all subsequent choices on that. To improve your decision-making skills, you must accept your first reaction isn't always the best one. Sometimes, it might lead you to jump to conclusions and make the wrong choices. Imagine being a surgeon who's operating on someone and needs to take a quick life-or-death decision: Wouldn't you want to take a few seconds to reflect before doing anything? I guess so. The ability to stop, even for a few milliseconds, is paramount to rewire your brain and consider various options.

Research has discovered that postponing your decision by as little as 50–100 milliseconds is already enough to let your brain focus on the relevant elements of the problem and eliminate distractions or useless information (*Making a Big Decision? Why You Should Take a (Quick) Pause Beforehand*, 2014). Studies have tried to analyze participants' response time to stimuli. Researchers either told them to respond as quickly as possible or as accurately as possible. When participants had to be accurate, they waited for a few more milliseconds before answering, even if they weren't always aware of that. When researchers compared their answers to the ones produced when responding as quickly as possible, they found out participants made fewer mistakes. Consequently, studies have confirmed taking a few more milliseconds to reflect can help us make more accurate decisions (*Making a Big Decision? Why You Should Take a (Quick) Pause Beforehand*, 2014).

You might not be aware of how important pausing can be because you don't even notice all the insignificant decisions you make every day. Just consider all the times you've crossed the road. Have you always been careful and looked for cars on your right and left? Being careless or in a rush can induce you to make the wrong decision and cross the road when a car is close. When we make fast decisions, we don't have accurate information. We consider similar past experiences and calculate what might happen next approximately. If you've crossed the road in a rush in the past, you might believe you can do it again. However, you can't be 100% sure this time you'll achieve the same results. Whenever you're about to make a decision rapidly, consider the above scenario. When you have to reply to a colleague or your significant other, you might not think that it's a life-or-death situation, so you might decide to give up on your impulses and not consider their feelings and thoughts. If you rethink your reactions to everyday events, you empower yourself to improve.

You can make a fast decision even when you have more than just a few seconds. For instance, you might have to make a paramount decision for your business and have a few days to consider various options. If you let fear, haste, and stress control your life, you might make the wrong choice. You might spend your days worrying without considering concrete options and then use your intuition to make the final decision. As useful as your gut feeling might be in certain situations, you must rely on more accurate information to make important choices. When you don't know what to do, take some time for yourself. Just relax and do something you enjoy to free your mind from your worries. Next, take a step back and analyze all the alternatives you have and the pros and cons. If you can't decide on your own, you can ask for help from your mentors, friends, and people you trust. You don't have to fight all your battles by yourself. They might not give you the answer you're looking for, but they help you analyze the problem from a different perspective and think of new options.

How can you make sure you pause before acting? You can start by acknowledging the importance of taking a break and allowing yourself to do it. When you don't know what to do, when you're not sure you really need something, and when you have many things to do at the same time, just accept that you need a pause. Acknowledge you have a desire and step back from it. You must always give yourself some time to focus on other things than the decision you have to make. Avoid spending all your days and nights fixating on it because it will only delay the final choice and won't help you accurately assess the problem. If you can't get rid of your desire, you must write it down somewhere, possibly in a journal. This way, you acknowledge and accept its importance and get it out of your mind to visualize it better. Do you feel like doing something about it? Do you want to eliminate that desire? Reflect on the actions you would like to undertake to move on with your life. If you feel motivated enough to act on your desire, just let some more time pass. If the urge comes back, it's not an urge anymore because you've already analyzed it a few times and you should do something about it. The above practice will help you get rid of all the urges that don't improve your life and elaborate on the ones that might be important to you. You can try the activity when you have to make a small decision, for example, before going to a shop to buy new clothes or if you should call someone or not.

TECHNIQUES TO PRACTICE TAKING A MOMENT BEFORE REACTING

In the previous section, we focused on things you can do to avoid fast decisions in the long term. Now, we'll focus on what looks apparently impossible: Modify your behavior in the small amount of time you have between a stimulus and your impulsive reaction. If you work on yourself and the ability to pause, you can choose to respond to events more effectively. You can try two useful activities to practice taking a moment: STOP and Pause.

STOP is an easy-to-remember acronym that stands for Stop, Take breaths, Observe, and Proceed. When you're about to react impulsively, you must remember to stop and pause. To master this skill, you must integrate this activity into your daily life and practice it as many times as you can. For instance, take a pause in front of your laptop before answering emails. In the beginning, you might struggle because you feel the urge to react immediately. You can take advantage of those moments to analyze your reactions and identify the emails that make you react more negatively. To make sure you remember to pause, you can also use a sort of code, like drinking a glass of water or looking outside of a window. Try to choose an activity that can help you calm down and can be easily performed in various contexts. This way, you can use it before reacting to any situation. For instance, drink a glass of water before talking to a difficult colleague or before yelling at another driver in the middle of a trafficked street. If it becomes a habit, you can use it everywhere.

When you've managed to pause, you can take a few deep breaths. If you want, you can close your eyes and just focus on breathing the air in and out. The third step consists of observing your present state without judging it. You must analyze your feelings and thoughts and simply accept them. It might help you say something like, *I'm feeling stressed, but it's okay because I'm facing a difficult situation, and everyone would feel the same in my situation.* Whatever you repeat to yourself, you must highlight that you have every right to feel how you feel and all feelings are normal, even the most negative ones. After observing your thoughts and emotions, you can proceed with awareness. Now, you know how you feel and think, so you can decide what to do next. Do you want to act on your negative emotions or behave differently? How can you effectively face this situation? Choose how you prefer responding. Keep in mind to practice the above exercise regularly to master the ability to pause before reacting.

The other activity is called "Pause" and allows you to take a moment before responding. The first step of this technique starts from the stage of observation in the STOP method. Therefore, you observe and analyze what's happening inside you. Visualize your thoughts and feelings as a train that passes in front of you. You decide not to get on board. You must catch the nanosecond before your reaction to make the right choice. During that nanosecond, think about an action you can do to replace your impulsive behavior. Practice finding the perfect activity by trial and error. You can think about an action that can provoke a healthier reaction and try it in various contexts. If it doesn't work, you come up with a different solution. Take all the time you need to analyze your inner self, replace your unhealthy behavior, and respond.

The two above exercises are very similar, so you can try both and choose the one that makes you feel more comfortable and relaxed. Remember it will take some time to adjust your reaction to events and you'll probably make many mistakes along the way. You must accept your failures as a sign that you're trying to improve and succeed in your attempts. Every mistake is a step forward to replacing your impulsive reactions with healthy responses.

In this chapter, we analyzed impulsive behaviors and how we can overcome them by pausing before reacting. We learned the negative effects impulsivity can have in the short and long term and the origins of our instinctive behaviors. Next, we discovered the significance of pausing and dedicating some time to get away from the chaos of our daily lives. Waiting for just a few milliseconds before making a decision can already change the outcome. Finally, we looked at two useful activities we can practice to enhance our ability to take a moment before reacting. In the upcoming chapter, we'll look at another crucial element for balanced living and effective leadership: stress management.

6

E-EASE

> The truth is that stress doesn't come from your boss, your kids, your spouse, traffic jams, health challenges, or other circumstances. It comes from your thoughts about your circumstances.
>
> — ANDREW BERNSTEIN

According to some studies, Americans are among the most stressed population in the world (The American Institute of Stress, 2022). About 55% of Americans report feeling stressed during the day. But they're not the only ones, as the global average of those who are affected by stress is 35%. Stress can have serious negative effects on your mental and physical health in the short and long term. If you feel stressed, you must do everything in your power to properly manage it and feel more relaxed. In this chapter, you'll discover the relationship between emotional intelligence and stress. You'll also learn useful techniques to manage stress and how mastering them will enhance your leadership capabilities. Finally, you'll find quick methods to feel more relaxed.

THE IMPACT OF STRESS ON EI

Stress is a normal reaction that everyone experiences (Mind, 2022). Stressors are all those people, events, and things that originate a change or challenge that we fear to face. When a stressor occurs, our bodies naturally respond by making us feel stressed. This way, we increase our levels of attention and are prepared to overcome danger. This means stress is positive and helps us adapt to different situations. When you feel stressed, your body automatically activates the fight-or-flight response. Your autonomic nervous system gets ready to deal with the stressor in two ways: fighting the problem (the fight response) or running away from it (the flight response). Let's say you have an important meeting at work in a few hours and you feel stressed about it. If you decide to fight, you prepare yourself to face the situation by taking advantage of your higher levels of attention. If you prefer flying, you invent an excuse to avoid the meeting, like being sick (Mind, 2022).

Low levels of stress can be beneficial if they allow you to feel more energized to complete a task. Problems arise when stress becomes intense or lasts for prolonged periods (Cleveland Clinic, 2021). Acute stress manifests a few minutes or hours after a stressful situation and lasts for less than two weeks. Examples are bereavement or natural disasters, like earthquakes. Chronic stress lasts for much longer, might disappear for some time, and then comes back. It's common among people who feel a lot of pressure during their daily lives and find themselves in difficult situations, such as poverty. Acute and chronic stress aren't considered mental health disorders but they're certainly linked with our mental health. If you have a mental disease and struggle to cope with it, you might develop stress. At the same time, stress can worsen mental conditions and provoke anxiety and depression (Cleveland Clinic, 2021).

If you often suffer from stress, you might notice some recurring symptoms (Cleveland Clinic, 2021). You might feel more irritable and impatient than usual, overwhelmed, worried, anxious, nervous or afraid, lonely, and depressed. You might struggle to enjoy yourself and control your negative thoughts. Common physical reactions include frequent aches, fatigue, sleep problems, difficulty breathing, chest pain, and sweating. Stress can impair your everyday life in various ways, like hindering your ability to make decisions, concentrate, and remember things. You might often feel the need to cry and constantly feel like something bad is about to happen. You might also engage in unhealthy behavior, such as spending too much, withdrawing from your loved ones, abusing substances, or gambling (Cleveland Clinic, 2021). Although the above symptoms are pretty straightforward, there's no way to measure stress and clearly state whether someone suffers from it or not because it's subjective. You're the only one who can tell if you suffer from it and how severe you think it is. If you feel extremely overwhelmed by stress and tend to engage in unhealthy behaviors to fight it, like drinking alcohol or thinking about hurting yourself, I suggest you talk to a doctor.

Interestingly, research has found that stress also has an important relationship with emotional intelligence (Yamani et al., 2014). A study has analyzed the effects teaching EI can have on adolescents' levels of stress and discovered that the more they learned and practiced that skill, the more they reduced their stress. Therefore, EI can be considered a significant predictor of future development of stress. Other researchers have focused on occupational stress and found that workers with higher levels of EI were less likely to suffer from job-related stress and that highly emotionally intelligent managers developed more effective stress management techniques. The above results indicate that those with higher levels of such skills tend to feel less stressed (Yamani et al., 2014). They don't avoid challenges but face them with the right attitude because they don't feel as stressed about changes as those with lower levels of emotional intelligence. They're better able to adapt to new situations and find original coping mechanisms to fight stress. In turn, they also improve their relationship with themselves and the people around them. If you feel stressed, you might have many negative feelings and thoughts about your skills and qualities, and you might feel angrier and more irritable with others, thus hindering your relationship with them.

If you have high levels of emotional intelligence, you accept stress as a normal reaction and take advantage of it to fight difficult situations. You don't try to hide it or panic because of it but simply understand it's part of your daily life, as it is for everyone else in the world. You learn to live with it and move on without impairing your mental and physical health.

STRESS MANAGEMENT TECHNIQUES BENEFICIAL FOR EVERYONE

You can manage and reduce stress in various ways but the most effective techniques are mindfulness, deep breathing, and exercise.

Mindfulness

In the previous section, we discussed the importance of pausing to stop engaging in impulsive behavior. We analyzed the importance of silence and connecting to our inner selves. An effective practice for learning to slow down and manage stress is mindfulness, which is an ancient technique that goes back centuries ago when Indian Buddhists first talked about it (Wooll, 2022b). Although the concept is connected to religion, it goes beyond the mere distinction of faiths and transcends cultural lines. In fact, mindfulness can improve everyone's life and should be practiced by all of us, independently from our religion and culture. Mindfulness focuses on allowing you to be present in the here and now, accept all your thoughts and emotions, pay attention to what happens inside and outside of you, and let go of past and future worries. In other words, mindfulness teaches you to give importance to every single moment of your life and appreciate who you are and what you have (Wooll, 2022b).

This practice isn't about exercise but is a lifestyle you can learn to improve your mental and physical health. If you've already heard about it, you might believe it consists of meditating as much as possible, but that's not true. Meditation is only one of the ways to become more mindful, as you can in all aspects of your life and through countless techniques. To understand what mindfulness entails, think about its opposite, which is being on autopilot. If you do things automatically, you don't think about them but worry about what you have to do next. Your mind is full of thoughts that don't focus on the present. When you're on autopilot, you don't pay attention to the people and things that surround you, thus forgetting about all the positive events that occur to you. For example, you might not notice how amazing your neighborhood is when you rush to work with your car or you might not pay attention to a nice gesture your significant other does to you.

Mindfulness can have numerous benefits on your physical and mental health. It allows you to focus on the most important things in your life and let go of the negative thoughts that impair your personal and professional success. In addition, it helps you focus and memorize your tasks more easily, thus making you more productive at work. It also makes you more flexible and allows you to adapt to changes without difficulty. Among the benefits, reducing stress is certainly one of the most relevant. If you become more mindful, you take advantage of every moment and stop worrying about the past or the future, thus feeling less stressed and more relaxed.

Mindfulness practices are varied and can be complex. Their main objective is to help you become aware and control your physical reactions and thoughts. The easiest exercises involve focusing on your breathing and body. First, find a comfortable place where you can sit or lie down and won't be disturbed. Next, set an alarm for five or more minutes, depending on how much time you feel like dedicating to the exercise. In the beginning, I suggest you start with two to five minutes. Then, choose a comfortable position and concentrate on your body: Feel what your feet, legs, arms, shoulders, neck, and head are feeling. Become aware of all your physical sensations. After focusing on your body for a few seconds, you can divert your attention to your breath. Feel the air breathing into your nose and out from your mouth. Finally, notice when your mind starts wandering. Don't judge yourself or obsess over the content of your thoughts but let go of them by accepting them. Acknowledge you have negative thoughts like anybody else, be kind to yourself, and move on with the activity. The above exercise is just an example of how mindfulness works, but you can try many more techniques.

Deep Breathing

As you previously learned, stress can provoke breathing difficulties, thus meaning one of the most effective techniques to relieve it is to learn to control your breathing. Breathing exercises are also connected with mindfulness because becoming aware of the way you breathe can help you control your physical reactions. You might have noticed when you feel stressed or anxious that you take shorter and more rapid breaths while you take deep and long ones when you feel relaxed.

A popular exercise to control your breathing is called the "4-7-8 breathing." Thanks to it, you make your body relax, fall asleep more easily, and reset after prolonged periods of study or work. This exercise is extremely easy and you can repeat it all the times you want during the day. First, find a comfortable and quiet place and a position you can maintain for a few minutes. Second, inhale with your nose to a count of four. Third, hold your breath for seven seconds, and finally, exhale to a count of eight. Repeat the above cycle about four times.

When you find yourself in stressful situations, you might over breathe. Deep breathing allows you to reduce stress and calm your body and mind. First, lie down in a comfortable place and breathe normally. Second, inhale deeply and exhale fully and slowly until you perceive your lungs empty. Focus on your abdomen instead of your chest to breathe. It might be helpful to imagine your stomach as a balloon that fills with air and then empties. Repeat the exercise for all the times you feel comfortable. In the beginning, I suggest you set an alarm for five minutes, as the activity might be intense.

Exercise

You might have often heard the importance of physical activity to improve your mental and physical health. When you practice an exercise, your brain produces the neurotransmitters called endorphins, which are responsible for making you feel good and improving your mood. In other words, practicing physical activity makes you happier and more excited. In addition, concentrating on the rhythms of your movements and the physical effort you make reduces stress because you focus on your body and forget about your mind for a while. Interestingly, you might experience the same benefits of meditation while working out. Physical activity has both short and long-term effects, as you immediately feel better after finishing an exercise, and your mood continues to improve until you have more positive feelings than negative ones (Madell, 2020).

If you're not used to exercising, you might wonder where you can start. The recommended amount of weekly physical activity is 150 minutes or about two hours and a half (Madell, 2020). The most effective way of exercising is doing it regularly for short periods. Therefore, practice physical activity for about 30 minutes every day for five days a week. In addition, you can split the 30 minutes into three different sessions, thus exercising for about 10 minutes every time. If you've rarely practiced physical activity, I suggest you start smaller. For example, you can set a goal to exercise for about one hour and a half a week, working out for 15 minutes every day for 6 days per week.

Some exercises can help you with stress more than others, like biking, dancing, brisk walking, swimming, playing tennis, and rowing. The essential element is you choose something you enjoy doing. If you don't like playing tennis, don't do it. Otherwise, you'll associate physical activity with negative emotions and might decide to stop practicing. If you don't feel comfortable starting with specific sports, you can try gardening or taking the stairs rather than the elevator. They're already a form of physical activity that can improve your mood.

HOW MANAGING STRESS ENHANCES LEADERSHIP CAPABILITY

In the last years, many leaders have been put under a lot of pressure, thus feeling more stressed than they've ever been. Research confirms that anxiety, depression, and burnout continue to increase among leaders (Positive, n.d.). Forty-one percent report feeling stressed, while almost forty percent indicate feeling exhausted. About 70% of leaders believe their levels of stress are seriously affecting their decision-making skills and 69% often consider quitting their job because of the negative effects their jobs have on their overall well-being. Most executives agree that their main concern is workload, but some of them also worry about fast internal changes and lack of career progress. Interestingly, the leaders who reported higher levels of stress were also those who didn't promote honest and open communication inside their company, felt less resilient, and felt less compassionate toward others. Therefore, executives with low levels of emotional intelligence are also the ones who struggle more with stress (Positive, n.d.).

If you want to improve your leadership skills and reduce the mental and physical effects of stress, you can try the activities discussed in the previous section. Alternatively, you can follow some specific tips. First, you must become aware of the physical sensations that precede stressful situations. If you know the warning signs, you can decide what to do about them. In particular, you must dedicate some time just to yourself to calm down and empty your mind. A few minutes alone in your office might already be enough. Remember to focus on positive things that make you smile, like looking at pictures with your friends, calling your significant other, or simply writing down your physical sensations. Another tip you can follow is to stop aiming for perfection. Most leaders set their main goal to be perfect and never make mistakes. However, such a goal is unattainable. Let yourself and your team members make errors and learn from them, as they will be paramount to improving the company. To reduce stress, you must accept you can control some things and not others. For instance, you can't expect never to make a mistake. Once you understand the difference, let go of all the things you can't control and move on. Dwelling on the past won't improve your mental health or your company.

To become a stress-free leader, you must also learn to appreciate all efforts and successes, even the smallest ones. Celebrate your daily victories with your employees or team members to feel more relaxed and boost your relationships. Some executives don't realize the importance of small achievements because they only look at the big picture and push their employees to always do more. Conversely, you must learn to pause and praise everyone's small steps toward the common goal, even yours. Finally, ask for help if you need it. If you're in a leadership position, you might believe you have to do everything on your own. However, this means increasing your workload and hindering your mental health.

Learn to delegate the less important and urgent tasks that other people from your team can handle just as well. Asking for help isn't a weakness but a way to share your burdens with people who can support you in achieving your goals. Collaboration is essential both among your employees and between you and your team members.

If you put into practice the above advice, you'll become a better leader and will immediately notice all the benefits. Research has found that less tense leaders are more likely to predict future complications and act rapidly to mitigate them. They also have more productive meetings with their employees and team members because they foster open and honest communication. Finally, leaders with low levels of stress improve their performance by saving time and effort and making more objective and timely observations about their team members and work (Positive, n.d.). If you've ever felt paralyzed because you felt so stressed you couldn't make decisions, you know what I'm talking about. Overthinking the past or future won't help you become an effective and emotionally intelligent leader.

QUICK AND LONG-TERM STRESS-RELIEF METHODS

There are countless ways in which you can relieve stress in your daily life. You don't have to put a lot of effort or invest much time into taking care of your mental health, as a few minutes will be enough.

You can control your facial expressions by forcing a laugh or smile, which can improve your mood quickly. You can also change your posture if you notice that you're slouching or sing a song that makes you feel happy. Alternatively, switch off your notifications on your smartphone for a while or give someone you love a hug. Acknowledge your stress instead of fighting or avoiding it. Some people might feel ashamed of their stress or convince themselves they're not truly stressed, but that's not a good way to improve their mood. That's why you must accept that you feel stressed and analyze where it comes from. Can you attribute it to a specific problem? Is it something you can solve in a little time? Reflect on it and think about solutions. Even when you're at work, try some easy activities, like stretching for a few minutes, changing positions at your desk, or taking a short walk. You can also do some physical exercise that doesn't require a lot of effort, like using a stress ball.

In general, an effective technique to de-stress is to take a walk. Whenever you can, try to replace driving or taking the elevator with going by foot. In addition, write down what you feel stressed about. Keeping a journal might seem uncomfortable or useless, but it can actually improve your mood and help you become more self-aware. You can report the physical and emotional sensations associated with your stress and keep track of the progress you make to manage negative feelings. If you have a bit more time, take a long and warm bath at the end of the day or clean up. Keeping your desk and house clean allows you to free your mind and improves your mood. If you don't manage to de-stress on your own, you can ask for help from a friend or someone you trust. Talking it out can already have positive effects on your mental health. Moreover, it helps you understand you're not the only one who has plenty of responsibilities and struggles to handle stress. In fact, people close to you are likely to feel the same way.

A long-term technique to manage stress and improve your mental health consists of taking care of yourself. Self-care is often mistakenly identified as selfishness or luxury, but it's necessary to increase your overall well-being. In particular, self-care reduces stress, anxiety, and burnout, improves your happiness, and boosts your relationships. If you take care of yourself, you're more likely to improve your behavior with others, who will feel more comfortable interacting with you. Self-care also prevents disease and helps you cope with illness (Scott, 2020). Taking care of yourself can have different meanings, as it refers to doing all the activities that put a smile on your face and make you feel cared for. There are three main types of self-care: physical, emotional, and spiritual (Lawler, 2023). Physical self-care includes taking care of your body by practicing physical activity, increasing your sleep quality, and eating healthier food. Emotional self-care focuses on giving importance to your emotions and involves practicing self-affirmations, saying "No" to the things you don't want to do or don't like, and taking breaks. Spiritual self-care connects you with your inner self in various ways, such as attending religious services, meditating, spending time in nature, or practicing daily acts of kindness (Lawler, 2023).

To make self-care effective, you must integrate it into your everyday activities. If you don't know where to start, you can follow some easy steps. First, write down all the things you like doing that bring you joy, energize you, and restore your balance. They can be calling your best friend weekly, booking a massage monthly, or spending more time outside. When you've found some activities, decide which one you would like to try first. Remember that you must start small if you want to successfully incorporate self-care into your daily life. Therefore, focus on one activity that doesn't require much time and won't affect your normal routine. Next, try practicing that behavior regularly for one week and reflect on how it makes you feel. Repeat the activity for a few more weeks, then get back to the list you wrote down when you started and choose another one. Getting support from your loved ones might help you achieve your goals. For example, you can share your plans and progress with them.

What are some common self-care practices? If you have one minute or less, you can simply drink a glass of water, accept to help someone, or accept an offer of help. Staying hydrated is paramount to reducing fatigue and anxiety, while supporting or being supported can improve your mood and make you feel more relaxed. Alternatively, you can give up on something you think you should do even if you don't want to. Think about your daily tasks and eliminate those you complete just because others think you should do them. Do you keep your house perfectly tidy because order and organization make you feel better or because you want to make a good impression? If you have a few more minutes, you can write down three things you're grateful for every day, plan a vacation, or take the first few steps to do something you really want to do.

In this chapter, we discovered the negative effects stress can have on our emotional intelligence and how to manage it.

We learned stress is a normal reaction and can be beneficial if it's not acute or chronic. In addition, people who have higher levels of emotional intelligence are more likely to feel less stressed. If we want to reduce stress, we can practice mindfulness, deep breathing exercises, or some sort of physical activity. Next, we discovered how becoming less stressed leaders can boost our emotional intelligence skills and companies. If we need some concrete and more practical advice on how to manage stress, the last section provides plenty of examples of quick exercises that can improve our stress levels in the long run. At this point, we analyzed almost every letter of the FOCUSED framework. The last one left is D: Deep relationships. In the next chapter, we'll delve into how managing stress effectively can pave the way for deeper, more meaningful relationships in both personal and professional life.

7

D-DEEP RELATIONSHIPS

> I've learned that people will forget what you said, people will forget what you did, but people will never forget how you made them feel.
>
> — MAYA ANGELOU

The above quote by Maya Angelou captures the essence of emotional intelligence perfectly. If you want to improve your relationships and create meaningful connections, you must put emotions first. Sooner or later, everyone will forget the good or bad things you said and did, but nobody will ever forget the sensations you made them feel. In other words, people will remember your level of emotional intelligence, how you express yourself, and how you value others. In this chapter, you'll discover the role EI plays in interpersonal relationships and how deep connections help in work settings. In the end, you'll also find useful suggestions on how to apply emotional intelligence in various types of relationships.

EI IN INTERPERSONAL RELATIONSHIPS

Emotional intelligence is the secret ingredient to building long-lasting intimate relationships. If you look for mutual kindness, soulful caring, real commitment, and deep intimacy, becoming more emotionally intelligent can help you reach your goals. EI can boost friendships because it promotes care and support between two individuals, which means they know each other's internal world, preferences, and dislikes. They trust each other and aren't afraid of expressing their true selves in front of the other. Consequently, they establish a deep connection that will probably accompany them for the rest of their lives. Emotional intelligence also enhances deep respect among friends or couples. For instance, you feel deep admiration toward your partner and vice versa if you're both highly emotionally intelligent. You hold them in high regard and appreciate all their flaws and qualities, failures and achievements, as they do with you. You also show your deep respect regularly with words and kind gestures.

Another aspect of your relationships that is deeply affected by emotional intelligence is communication. Research has found that the first three minutes of a conversation are paramount to determining the outcome (Bisignano, 2018). If the discussion starts harshly, it is likely to end abruptly. If you're emotionally intelligent, you know how to express your thoughts and feelings without hurting others, thus increasing your chances of having an open and positive interaction with your loved ones. You know when it's the right time to talk about a delicate topic and how to face it. You also avoid criticism and contempt because you're aware they won't help you achieve what you want from your conversations with others. A direct consequence of open and positive communication is conflict management. If you're emotionally intelligent, you solve conflicts effectively. You're aware we can all have different opinions and disagree on important topics, even with our significant others or best friends. Therefore, you accept you're different from your loved ones and try to understand their point of view. Emotional intelligence doesn't lead you to face fewer conflicts but to react appropriately. For instance, couples who are highly intelligent don't argue less often than others but they know how to reach compromises while respecting each other's ideas. Therefore, they're more likely to end conflicts successfully.

Emotional intelligence also has a positive impact on maintaining a healthy relationship. In fact, it allows you to distinguish between yourself and your partner or best friend, thus encouraging separate identities even in the deepest and closest connections. When you start a new relationship, you don't become the person others want you to be but remain authentic to yourself. You understand your role inside your relationships and respect it. At the same time, you acknowledge your identity inside the couple as part of a team of two people. In addition, emotional intelligence allows the development of healthy boundaries between you and your loved ones. As you acknowledge your identity is different from others, you're aware of what you like and don't like in a relationship and you're not afraid to tell it to your partner or best friend. If something makes you feel uncomfortable, you say it and gently ask others to stop engaging in behaviors that make you feel that way. If you're emotionally intelligent, you don't only set clear boundaries with your partner or friend but also between you two and your other relationships. Even if you find yourself in the best romantic relationship you ever had, you remember your family and friends, as they're also important. You keep in touch with them and try to maintain contact, even if it is different from when you were single. At the same time, you don't neglect your significant other to dedicate all your time and energy to your family, friends, and other loved ones.

Thanks to emotional intelligence, you can also share your life to create deep connections. Even if you know there are divergences between you and your loved ones, you just accept them and don't focus on them. You dedicate yourself to staying connected to the ones you love and do activities you enjoy together. If you and your best friend enjoy going to the cinema, you take the time to organize a night out and watch a movie you both like. Building strong and deep relationships requires time, effort, and commitment. Even if you've been together with your partner for decades or known your best friend since you were very little, you must dedicate yourself to them and improve your connections. Emotional intelligence makes you understand you must take care of your relationships from the beginning to the end and never take someone for granted.

At this point, you might believe EI is essential to foster positive and healthy connections, and you're right. However, this doesn't mean lacking this skill automatically leads you to end your relationships abruptly. If you're willing to improve and both you and your loved one are committed to making it work, then the situation can get better. Moreover, lacking emotional intelligence in specific relationships can be a sign that the other person lacks this skill, too. You can spot EI in others by following some easy tips. First, they talk about their emotions and try to explain how and why they feel. Second, they are open-minded and curious about you. They observe your behavior without judging, make considerations, and discuss them with you respectfully because they want to understand everything about you. Third, they know how to meet their needs. If they feel hungry, they don't get angry or snappy around you but they understand they have to satisfy their need for food. This is just an example of being aware of physical and emotional sensations that can impact others. Then, emotionally intelligent people have clear boundaries in all their relationships, meaning they're able to say "No" when they want to. Finally, having long-lasting relationships is a good sign of high emotional intelligence. If your partner or friend is close to their family or has friendships that have lasted for decades, they're more likely to know what works and what doesn't inside different types of relationships. Consequently, they've spent time developing their EI.

HOW EI SKILLS IMPROVE WORK RELATIONS AND TEAM DYNAMICS

After discussing emotional intelligence in interpersonal relationships, let's focus on work and team dynamics. Employee relations refer to the relationship between employees and employers (Verlinden, 2020). The ultimate goal of employee relations is to build positive and open interactions inside a company. In some cases, a specific team is responsible for managing relationships while in others, employee relations consist of policies and plans designed to boost connections. In any case, the human resources department usually oversees them. Employee relations cover all dimensions of the relationship between employee and employer, from the emotional to the contractual one. They involve supporting employees, addressing their concerns, promoting mutual respect and trust, and developing a strong company culture and positive work environment.

If you're the leader, you must value employee relations for various reasons. First, they boost open and healthy communication in the workplace, thus reducing misunderstandings and conflicts. Second, they increase employees' morale and loyalty, which leads to higher levels of productivity and employee retention. Third, you develop a better reputation as an employer because your employees speak highly of you. Consequently, customers, investors, and possible future employees will be more likely to collaborate with you. Finally, employee relations improve organizational performance because employees feel inspired and committed to pursuing the company's long-term goals. Even if you're not a leader but a member of a team, understanding team dynamics is fundamental to achieving your goals at work and improving your emotional intelligence. Team dynamics include efforts to coordinate, communicate, and collaborate to achieve the same objectives and they're influenced by personality traits, work styles, the company culture, and the organizational structure.

Emotional intelligence is particularly helpful in three work-related aspects: conflict resolution, communication, and collaboration, as we'll discover in the next sections.

Conflict Resolution

A conflict occurs when two people disagree and can't find a common ground. The main causes might be misunderstandings or different opinions, interests, and morals. Before looking at how you can manage conflicts effectively using emotional intelligence, you must understand not all arguments are bad and you don't have to intervene at all times. Conflicts are inevitable because we all have different opinions and different perspectives on the same topic. You mustn't focus on eliminating all sources of arguments but facing them properly. As a team leader, you're not forced to placate a conflict every time it happens. Sometimes, it might be more useful to let team members handle arguments on their own to improve their communication skills.

To use emotional intelligence to handle conflicts, you must understand your team members first. Get to know each one of them and investigate their personalities, values, and traits. This way, you'll have an idea of how they might react when conflicts arise. Next, you must encourage everyone to express their emotions as clearly as possible. They don't have to say things like, "I feel angry," but go deeper and explain how they feel and why. They should say something like, "I feel frustrated because you chose another team member to present this important project." If they learn to express their emotions with you, they're more likely to do the same with the other team members when arguments arise. In addition, you must address conflicts calmly and privately. If two members have a disagreement, talk to them in a room where the others can't see or hear you, as conflicts can get worse if everyone feels involved. Last but not least, remember to always be a good role model for your team. If you show others you're able to regulate your emotions and solve conflicts effectively, they'll try to do the same.

Communication

Open communication among team members is an essential element in solving conflicts properly and promoting deep relationships. As already mentioned in the previous section, the most effective way of dealing with arguments is to foster a positive work environment and be a good role model. If you show your team members you're not afraid of expressing your thoughts and emotions and respect them, they're more likely to follow your lead. You mustn't feel ashamed when talking about your emotions. After all, leaders have feelings, just like anybody else. You can get angry, feel relaxed, celebrate a success, or feel sad. Once you express how you feel, ask your team members to do the same and make sure they don't feel judged by you or their colleagues. Practically, you can organize one-on-one meetings, open feedback sessions, and team-building exercises. You can include them in your daily routine so that team members get used to sharing their thoughts and feelings.

When discussing conflict resolution, we mentioned understanding your team members. If you want to build open and healthy communication, you must also recognize their communication styles. This way, you'll know how and when to answer their requests and thoughts. For instance, you can analyze your team members' behaviors and identify if they prefer talking face-to-face in front of everyone or just with you or if they favor written communication. More specifically, you can study the four essential communication styles: Passive, aggressive, passive-aggressive, and assertive. If you realize some of your team members are assertive, encourage them to show how they communicate their wants and needs to others. If you notice someone is aggressive, passive-aggressive, or passive, make them understand that's not the most effective way of getting their needs met. At the same time, you must teach them you're ready to actively listen to them if they put effort into improving their communication skills.

Collaboration

Solving conflicts effectively and fostering healthy communication lead to enhanced collaboration among the team members. If they feel free to express their thoughts and emotions and they feel safe because they know you'll do your best to find a compromise that benefits everyone, they'll be more likely to collaborate with each other and with you. To foster cooperation, you must encourage your team members to get to know each other well. They shouldn't just focus on work and the projects they have to submit but discuss how they feel, what they do outside of work, if they have some hobbies, and so on. The simplest way to build deep relationships is by encouraging small talk and simple interactions among your team members. Let them discuss what they did the night before or during the weekend and how they enjoy spending their days. Let them talk about their past, what they studied, where they worked, and how they found themselves in previous workplaces. The more they investigate, the more they discover about each other.

Letting your team members discuss their lives outside of work might seem useless but it can actually help them understand who they're working with, if they can trust them, and how they work. For instance, they might learn how fast the other members are at completing tasks, if they struggle to collaborate with others and tend to work by themselves, how they value the quality of their work, and what physical and emotional energy they have. If they had a rough day at home, would they be able to complete the assigned projects or would they need some time to themselves? The more each member knows about the others, the more they're ready to face all sorts of obstacles inside the team and collaborate to pursue the same goals. You can foster cooperation by providing small but difficult projects to complete together to challenge them and make them overcome problems together. Finally, you can encourage time spent together outside of work by providing opportunities to meet and have fun outside the company walls. You mustn't limit yourself to valuing and improving your relationship with team members but must also encourage deep connections among them.

GUIDELINES FOR USING EI TO MAINTAIN AND IMPROVE RELATIONSHIPS

You can follow some specific guidelines to use emotional intelligence in your daily interactions with others. In the following sections, we'll look at the various types of relationships and how you can apply emotional intelligence to each one.

Couples

If you or your partner lack emotional intelligence, you can work together to improve the situation. In particular, you can try three useful activities. The first one involves writing down a list of miscommunications or negative behaviors that destabilize or threaten your partner. Then, you add what you really mean by behaving that way for each specific action. For instance, you might have a very long bath every once in a while, flirt with someone else, lose your temper suddenly, or stay on your phone for prolonged periods. Your significant other might not understand why you engage in such negative behaviors and you might risk hindering your relationships. Even if you think your actions have obvious reasons or that your partner should understand why you do certain things, you must put effort into explaining your reasons. You might take a long bath or stay on the phone if you feel angry about something they did but don't know how to tell them. Alternatively, you might flirt with someone else because you believe they don't give you the attention and care you deserve.

The second activity consists of recalling past grudges. Becoming emotionally withdrawn for no apparent reason is a sign of emotional mismanagement or fear of expressing certain needs. Thanks to this exercise, you can become more aware of your and your partner's emotions and how you deal with them. Now, try to recall a situation when you held a grudge to your significant other and answer the following questions:

- Why did you get upset?
- How did you feel?
- Why did you struggle to discuss the problem out loud?
- In your opinion, what is the reason behind your difficulty in directly talking about the problem?

The last exercise to improve your emotional intelligence inside your couple concerns reflecting on your past, especially your childhood and how your parents communicated. To better understand certain behavioral patterns, you must become aware of how your parents behave and influence your perception of communication inside the relationship. Answer the following questions:

- What did you learn from your parents about communication inside the couple?

- What did they use to do when they felt upset?
- What were your role models as a child?
- What did your parents allow you to do when you felt upset or angry?

If you want, you can practice the above activities by yourself first to become more aware of yourself. When you feel comfortable, you can propose the same exercises to your partner and let them do them by themselves or complete them together.

Families

Have you ever had a misunderstanding with a family member, like your mother, sibling, or cousin? Families should be our closest allies, and yet we might often struggle to communicate our emotions and thoughts effectively, thus causing conflicts. As closed relationships are centered around feelings, enhancing your emotional intelligence is the best tool you can use to improve your communication inside your family. First, learn to take care of yourself first. If you neglect your self-care, you won't be able to care for your loved ones and interact with them effectively. The more time and energy you dedicate to your family, the more you must allocate some time to yourself, too. Most families also complain about lack of communication and members often wonder why others don't listen to them. The majority of the time, the reason is because they don't listen to their loved ones. Practice active listening and learn to listen carefully before talking. To build a positive and safe environment, you must also make all members understand feelings are always okay but we all have the power to choose how to behave. Therefore, everyone has the right to feel angry or sad, but they also have the tools to choose between closing themselves off and engaging in unhealthy behaviors or making an effort to share their emotions and thoughts.

No matter your role inside the family—you must give and receive at the same time. If you don't give, you might struggle to receive, and if you don't receive, you might have little to give. Make sure you balance what you give and what you receive, as all other family members should do. Another common issue involves solving problems for others. You might feel protective toward your family members, especially younger or older ones, and you might want to help them in all possible ways. However, that's not what they need. They must make their own mistakes and learn what's best for them. Don't give them unsolicited advice or take charge of their problems, as they might react negatively. In most cases, your loved ones only need someone to vent with and talk openly to. To take care of your family, you must also learn to apologize and acknowledge your errors. This is especially important when you interact with younger members, like your children, and you make a mistake that causes them negative emotions. Even the best parent in the world can make an error, so there's nothing to feel ashamed of. The most important aspect is that you admit your mistake in front of your children and apologize. This way, you not only model emotional integrity and humility, but you also prove that everyone can learn at any age.

To improve your relationships inside the family, you mustn't take everyone's needs for granted. This is particularly true for your children, who will grow up much faster than you can imagine. Therefore, they'll rapidly change their needs and won't always keep you informed of what they want. It's your responsibility to ask them if this year they need something different from the previous one. For instance, your children might need your advice when they're 12 and stop talking to you when they turn 13 because they need to learn on their own. Don't take it personally, as it's normal behavior —just accept they've changed. The same is true even for older members who might have different needs at different ages. Last but not least, you mustn't neglect any family member. Those who demand the most emotional attention might get more, while those who don't might give the impression they don't need others to show them love and affection. However, that's not true, as every member needs to know they're loved. Never forget to show equal affection to all your family.

Parent–Child

In the previous section, we started discussing some useful tips to boost your relationship with your children and now we'll look at some more. Especially when they're very little, you might struggle to understand their reasons and try to use logic to fight their battles. However, it won't help you understand your children's wants and needs. If you have a young kid, you might have found yourself in frustrating situations. For instance, you might have decided to prepare their favorite breakfast to surprise them. Then, you discovered they don't like it as much as they did a week ago and don't feel like eating it. According to logic, such behaviors don't make sense. That's why you must use awareness and empathy to understand what happens inside your children's minds.

If you want to become an emotionally intelligent parent, you must learn to take care of yourself first, as you already learned. Some parents find themselves overwhelmed by all their responsibilities and forget to dedicate some time to themselves, thus risking hindering their relationship with their kids because they're not fully focused and relaxed. If you realize your stress levels increase too much, just take a pause from everything and ask for someone's help. Let other family members, friends, or neighbors take care of your children while you take a day off to do something you enjoy and that improves your mood. To become an emotionally intelligent parent, you must also concentrate on enhancing your connection with your kids instead of fixating on results, performance, or duties. We're all extremely busy and have to do many things every day, but that doesn't mean we can't fully dedicate ourselves to our kids just for a few seconds or minutes. Asking them how their day was is already enough to show them you care about them and take the time to listen to them. Free your mind from all the thoughts you usually have and be fully present. Keep in mind quality is always better than quantity. When they become adults, your kids won't remember if you spent just a few minutes or a few hours every day with them during their childhood. However, they'll never forget the deep connection you've always tried to create.

Friends

Over your life, you might have developed different friendships. You might know people who you consider acquaintances, friends you feel close to, and best friends. How do they differ in your opinion? Why are some people just someone you know while others become lifelong friends? The main reason is emotional intelligence. Those who possess higher levels of EI are more likely to build strong and deep connections that will last for a lifetime. How can you be sure your best friend is emotionally intelligent? They probably have some specific traits.

First, they follow through and up. They always try to keep themselves informed of what goes on in your life and check up on you when they know you have an important upcoming event. They encourage you and give you the strength to face challenges before they occur. Then, they congratulate you and celebrate your success together or offer a shoulder to cry on if things don't go as you planned. They make sure you're okay and are there when you need their help. They do their best to maintain contact with you even if you live far away from each other. They might not have the possibility to meet you in person every now and then but they do their best to text you regularly, send you audio records to hear your voice, and video chat to see you.

Second, your best friend is not envious of your successes. If they're emotionally intelligent, they understand the importance of surrounding themselves with successful, good, and smart people. If you receive a promotion or finally start doing your dream job, they celebrate your achievements with you, even if they're in an unfavorable position. They know your successes are also theirs. Finally, one of the most common problems among friends is a lack of communication. You might feel like your friends are very busy and don't want to hear you vent about your bad day, so you might decide to keep your emotions to yourself. In the long run, such behaviors might impair your friendships. If you want to become an emotionally intelligent friend, you must share your emotions and thoughts. You mustn't be afraid of conflicts as they arise in all contexts and don't hinder your relationships if you solve them effectively. In other words, never stop talking to your friends and expressing what you have inside. If your friends are emotionally intelligent, they'll always have the time to listen to your worries and problems.

This chapter highlighted the significance of deep relationships to enhance our emotional intelligence. First, we looked at the role EI has in interpersonal relationships and how it can help us build strong and deep connections that will last for years. Next, we learned the importance of EI in professional relationships, especially if we're leaders. We must foster a positive work environment where everyone feels free to express their emotions and thoughts if we want to reduce conflicts among team members, improve communication, and promote collaboration. Finally, we looked at practical guidelines to practice and enhance our levels of emotional intelligence in all aspects of our lives: romantic relationships, family, children, and friendships. At this point, we have a clear understanding of all the letters of the FOCUSED framework and know how to put what we've learned into practice. The last thing left is to take action and improve our relationships and decision-making skills.

CONCLUSION

Until a few years ago, people thought their cognitive intelligence and talent were the two main tools they needed to succeed in life and become effective leaders. If they were good at something and smart enough, then they were destined to improve their relationships and climb the ladder. However, research has recently disproved the above theory and found another element that predicts our future successes: emotional intelligence. If we develop our levels of EI, we're capable of achieving our goals, feeling happier, and being satisfied with our personal and professional lives.

This book taught us everything we need to know through a theoretical and practical framework called FOCUSED. We looked at useful activities we can practice daily to enhance our levels of emotional intelligence at home and work. In the first chapter, we analyzed the letter F: Fundamentals. We learned emotional intelligence is an essential skill that includes self-awareness, self-management, social awareness, and relationship management. We must be aware of ourselves and how others perceive us, regulate our emotions, and improve our relationships if we want to become more emotionally intelligent. EI is particularly useful if we're leaders, aim at becoming leaders, or want to enhance our leadership skills. In fact, the factor that distinguishes effective leaders from all others is their level of EI.

The second chapter discussed the letter O: Observation. It focused on the first element that composes emotional intelligence, which is self-awareness. To become more self-aware, we can practice some easy techniques, like discovering our strengths and weaknesses, increasing our focus, using our intuition, exercising self-discipline, and apologizing when necessary. The second chapter also showed us important past and present leaders who stand out for their high levels of EI. In Chapter 3, we analyzed the letter C: Communication. We didn't discuss communication in general but concentrated on a particular aspect of it that is often neglected: active listening. Listening is much more important than talking because it allows us to understand others' points of view and answer appropriately. We discovered some useful tips to enhance our active listening skills, like paying attention to our and others' nonverbal communication.

Chapter 4 analyzed the letter U: Understanding. If we want to become more emotionally intelligent, we must understand others or become more empathetic. Empathy is paramount both in our personal and professional lives because it improves our relationships. If we show empathy, we make others understand we care about their emotions and thoughts and value their opinions. Chapter 5 discussed the letter S: Slow down. It taught us the importance of fighting our impulsive behaviors to improve our mental health and relationships and make more conscious decisions. To overcome impulsivity, we must learn to take a pause before reacting. Even waiting a few milliseconds before responding to stressful situations can already change the outcome.

Chapter 6 showed us what the E means: Ease. We learned how stress can negatively affect our mental and physical health and useful techniques we can practice in our daily lives to control and reduce stress. Among the most common ones are mindfulness, which is an ancient practice that helps us stay focused on the present; deep breathing, which involves concentrating on how we breathe; and physical activity. We also discovered the importance of managing stress properly to become effective and successful leaders and practical tips to reduce stress, like taking a walk outside or calling a friend.

Finally, the last letter of the FOCUSED framework stands for Deep relationships. To become more emotionally intelligent, we must value our connections and make them deep and strong, not only in our personal lives but also in our professional ones. At work, we can improve our conflict management skills, promote open and honest communication, and encourage collaboration among team members. As leaders, we must know our employees' needs and wants and they must have time to get to know each other better, even outside of work. Finally, the last chapter taught us some essential guidelines we must follow to boost our relationships with our partners, families, children, and friends.

Thanks to the FOCUSED framework, you have the power to change your life for the better. You can build long-lasting and meaningful relationships with your colleagues and in your personal life. In addition, you can enhance your decision-making skills to become a more effective leader or improve your leadership skills. The FOCUSED framework gives you all the tools to become more emotionally intelligent. However, don't just try to understand EI—live it. Start practicing the techniques discussed in this book today and pave the way for stronger relationships and a more successful life.

HELLO!

We hope you've enjoyed your journey through "The Secret of Emotional Intelligence." Your insights and feedback are incredibly valuable to us and to future readers. If you've had a chance to explore the book, we kindly remind you to share your thoughts and experiences.

Leaving a review is simple, yet it makes a huge difference. You can post your feedback by scanning the QR code. Your honest opinion will help others discover the transformative power of emotional intelligence!

Thank you for being a part of our reading community.

Best Regards,
G. Gagliardi.

REFERENCES

Ackerman, C. (2020, April 1). *What is self-awareness and why is it important? [+5 ways to increase it]*. Positive Psychology. https://positivepsychology.com/self-awareness-matters-how-you-can-be-more-self-aware/

Agerbeck, B. (n.d.). *How to focus when you are listening*. Loosetooth.com. https://www.loosetooth.com/how-to-focus

The American Institute of Stress (2022). *What is stress?* https://www.stress.org/daily-life

Angelou, M. (2019). *A quote by Maya Angelou*. GoodReads. https://www.goodreads.com/quotes/5934-i-ve-learned-that-people-will-forget-what-you-said-people

Avendano, O. (2021, July 3). *Listening comprehension*. ToolsHero. https://www.toolshero.com/communication-methods/listening-comprehension/

Benefits of active listening. (2021, August 15). In Professional Development. https://www.inpd.co.uk/blog/benefits-of-active-listening

Bernstein, A. (2020, August 17). *55 best stress quotes*. Driven. https://home.hellodriven.com/articles/55-best-stress-quotes/

Bisignano, A. (2018, May 29). *Making love last: the importance of emotional intelligence*. Good Therapy. https://www.goodtherapy.org/blog/making-love-last-importance-of-emotional-intelligence-0601184

Blaschka, A. (2022, March 19). *5 reasons why the "power of the pause" is your secret career weapon*. Forbes. https://www.forbes.com/sites/amyblaschka/2022/03/19/5-reasons-why-the-power-of-the-pause-is-your-secret-career-weapon/?sh=4939575d3d07

Bradberry, T. (2014, January 9). *Emotional intelligence - EQ*. Forbes. https://www.forbes.com/sites/travisbradberry/2014/01/09/emotional-intelligence/?sh=6de46fda1ac0

Bradley, C. (2018, August 15). *The power of pause*. Mindful. https://www.mindful.org/the-power-of-pause/

Brower, T. (2021, September 19). *Empathy is the most important leadership skill according to research*. Forbes. https://www.forbes.com/sites/tracybrower/2021/09/19/empathy-is-the-most-important-leadership-skill-according-to-research/?sh=2709ecf23dc5

Butler, J. (2021, February 19). *The cost of misunderstanding*. Rest from Stress. https://jbpartners.com/lessons/the-cost-of-misunderstanding/#:~:

Case study - 27: emotional intelligence in corporate offices. (2022, October 15). Drishti IAS. https://www.drishtiias.com/ethics/case-studies/case-study-27-emotional-intelligence-in-corporate-offices

Channell, M. (2023, May 25). *How to apply emotional intelligence to conflict resolution in the workplace*. TSW Training. https://www.tsw.co.uk/blog/leadership-and-management/emotional-intelligence-for-conflict-resolution/

Cherry, K. (2023a, February 22). *Types of nonverbal communication*. Verywell Mind. https://www.verywellmind.com/types-of-nonverbal-communication-2795397

Cherry, K. (2023b, February 22). *What is empathy?* Verywell Mind. https://www.verywellmind.com/what-is-empathy-2795562

Cherry, K. (2023c, March 10). *What is self-awareness?* Verywell Mind. https://www.verywellmind.com/what-is-self-awareness-2795023

Cherry, K. (2023d, March 22). *How to be open-minded and why it matters*. Verywell Mind. https://www.verywellmind.com/be-more-open-minded-4690673

Cherry, K. (2023e, May 2). *Emotional intelligence: how we perceive, evaluate, express, and control emotions*. Verywell Mind. https://www.verywellmind.com/what-is-emotional-intelligence-2795423

Chia, S. (2021, February 3). *15 ways to improve your focus and concentration*. BetterUp. https://www.betterup.com/blog/15-ways-to-improve-your-focus-and-concentration-skills

Cleveland Clinic. (2021, January 28). *Stress*. https://my.clevelandclinic.org/health/articles/11874-stress

Cooks-Campbell, A. (2021, June 11). *50+ self-care practices to take better care of yourself*. BetterUp. https://www.betterup.com/blog/self-care-practices

Cooks-Campbell, A. (2023). *Triggered? Learn what emotional triggers are and how to deal with them*. BetterUp. https://www.betterup.com/blog/triggers

Cuncic, A. (2022, November 9). *What is active listening?* Verywell Mind. https://www.verywellmind.com/what-is-active-listening-3024343

Delfino, D. (2022, August 15). *Apologizing at work: when is it necessary?* Grammarly Blog. https://www.grammarly.com/blog/apologizing-at-work/

Dreher, B., & Nowak, C. (2019, October 31). *9 split-second decisions that changed history*. Reader's Digest. https://www.rd.com/list/split-second-decisions-changed-history/

Duggal, N. (2018, July 13). *Emotional intelligence in the workplace: why you need it, how to get it.* Simpli Learn. https://www.simplilearn.com/emotional-intelligence-what-why-and-how-article

Dutra, A. (2012, January 5). *The power of pause.* Harvard Business Review. https://hbr.org/2012/01/the-power-of-pause

8 key listening comprehension skills. (2017, April 3). Listenwise Blog. https://blog.listenwise.com/2017/04/8-components-listening/

Emeritus (2023, July 26). *How does emotional intelligence influence leadership effectiveness?.* https://emeritus.org/blog/leadership-emotional-intelligence-skills/#:~

Emotional intelligence in leaders: real life examples. (2016, November 11). Envision Global Leadership. https://envisiongloballeadership.com/blog/emotional-intelligence-leaders-real-life-examples/

Epictetus. (n.d.). *Epictetus quotes.* BrainyQuote. https://www.brainyquote.com/quotes/epictetus_106298

50 tips for improving your emotional intelligence. (2022, January 12). Roche Martin. https://www.rochemartin.com/blog/50-tips-improving-emotional-intelligence

Frankl, V. E. (n.d.). *Viktor E. Frankl quotes.* BrainyQuote. https://www.brainyquote.com/quotes/viktor_e_frankl_160380

Freiberg, K., & Freiberg, J. (2018, July 19). *Madiba leadership: 5 lessons nelson mandela taught the world about change.* Forbes. https://www.forbes.com/sites/kevinandjackiefreiberg/2018/07/19/madiba-leadership-5-lessons-nelson-mandela-taught-the-world-about-change/?sh=5323213141ba

Goleman, D. (n.d.). *A quote by Daniel Goleman.* Goodreads. https://www.goodreads.com/quotes/7137394-emotional-intelligence-accounts-for-80-percent-of-career-success

Hanna, R. (n.d.). *How can you use active listening to improve your feedback skills?* Linkedin. https://www.linkedin.com/advice/0/how-can-you-use-active-listening-improve-your

Hardy, D. (n.d.). *A quote by Darren Hardy.* Goodreads. https://www.goodreads.com/quotes/1339219-the-first-step-toward-change-is-awareness-if-you-want

Herrera, J. (2021, November 6). *Wellbeing begins with pausing.* We Thrive. https://wethrivewellbeing.com/wellbeing-begins-with-pausing/

Houston, E. (2019, February 6). *The importance of emotional intelligence (including EI quotes).* Positive Psychology. https://positivepsychology.com/importance-of-emotional-intelligence/#:~

How to effectively use active listening in the workplace. (2023, February 4). Indeed.

https://www.indeed.com/career-advice/career-development/listening-in-the-workplace

How to improve listening skills and why it's important. (2022, November 19). Indeed. https://ca.indeed.com/career-advice/career-development/how-to-improve-listening-skills

Jadhav, K. (2023, May 31). *Pause and reflect: the power of thoughtful decision-making.* LinkedIn. https://www.linkedin.com/pulse/pause-reflect-power-thoughtful-decision-making-kiran/

Jiménez, J. (2021, July 16). *Compassion vs. empathy: understanding the difference.* BetterUp. https://www.betterup.com/blog/compassion-vs-empathy

Kassel, G. (2018, December 3). *The handful of personality traits emotionally intelligent friends tend to share.* Well+Good. https://www.wellandgood.com/high-emotional-intelligence-signs-in-friend/

Khan, S. (2023, April 15). *Everyday leadership: why it should be inculcated in every person.* LinkedIn. https://www.linkedin.com/pulse/everyday-leadership-why-should-inculcated-every-person-shahid-khan/

Klaphaak, A. (2023, August 1). *How to identify your strengths and weaknesses.* WikiHow. https://www.wikihow.com/Identify-Your-Strengths-and-Weaknesses#Assessing-Your-Strengths-and-Weaknesses

Landry, L. (2019). *Why emotional intelligence is important in leadership.* Harvard Business School Online. https://online.hbs.edu/blog/post/emotional-intelligence-in-leadership

Lawler, M. (2023, March 17). *What is self-care and why is it so important for your health?* Everyday Health. https://www.everydayhealth.com/self-care/

Leadership stress management: strategies and benefits. (2022, October 7). Infopro Learning. https://www.infoprolearning.com/blog/leadership-stress-management-strategies-and-benefits/

Lee, H. (n.d.). *To kill a mockingbird: important quotes explained.* SparkNotes. https://www.sparknotes.com/lit/mocking/quotes/page/2/

Madell, R. (2020, March 27). *How to use exercise as a stress reliever.* Healthline. https://www.healthline.com/health/heart-disease/exercise-stress-relief

Making a big decision? Why you should take a (quick) pause beforehand. (2014, March 15). HuffPost. https://www.huffpost.com/entry/take-a-pause-before-decision_n_4936798

Miller, K. (2019, August 20). *50 practical examples of high emotional intelligence.* Positive Psychology. https://positivepsychology.com/emotional-intelligence-examples/

Mind. (2022, March). *What is stress?* https://www.mind.org.uk/information-support/types-of-mental-health-problems/stress/what-is-stress/

Mindful. (2018, December 12). *How to practice mindfulness.* https://www.mind ful.org/how-to-practice-mindfulness/

Moore, C. (2019, March 19). *Emotional intelligence in relationships - couples activi-ties.* Positive Psychology. https://positivepsychology.com/emotional-intelli gence-relationships/#3-emotional-intelligence-activities-for-couples

Morey, R. (2018, July 16). *How 5 emotionally intelligent ceos handle their power.* Pagely. https://pagely.com/blog/emotionally-intelligent-ceos/

Mulvania, P. (2020, September 18). *The importance of active listening.* Gift of Life Institute. https://www.giftoflifeinstitute.org/the-importance-of-active-listening/

Nguyen, E. (2021, December 28). How to spot emotional intelligence in a part-ner. *Refinery29.* https://www.refinery29.com/en-gb/emotional-intelligence-relationships

Nortje, A. (2021, February 4). *Empathy 101: 3+ examples and psychology defini-tions.* Positive Psychology. https://positivepsychology.com/empathy-psychology/

The pause technique: a powerfully simple 3-step decision-making approach. (2023, May 19). The Envisionary. https://www.theenvisionary.com/article/the-pause-technique-decision-making/

Perry, E. (2022a, January 12). *Understanding the difference between sympathy and empathy.* BetterUp. https://www.betterup.com/blog/empathy-vs-sympathy

Perry, E. (2022b, August 31). *7 types of listening that can change your life and work.* BetterUp. https://www.betterup.com/blog/types-of-listening

Pick, J. (2018, July 19). *Emotional intelligence and teamwork: how EQ helps your team.* Profiles. https://www.profilesasiapacific.com/2018/07/19/emotional-intelligence-and-teamwork/

Positive (n.d.). *Stress in leaders: what's driving it and what's the impact?.* https:// www.positivegroup.org/loop/articles/stress-in-leaders-whats-driving-it-and-whats-the-impact

Practicing pausing (STOP). (n.d.). UVAHealth Wisdom & Wellbeing Program. https://www.medicalcenter.virginia.edu/wwp/positive-practices-to-enhance-resilience-and-improve-interpersonal-communication-individ ual-techniques-1/self-regulation/practicing-pausing-stop/

The psychology of emotional and cognitive empathy. (n.d.). Lesley University. https://lesley.edu/article/the-psychology-of-emotional-and-cognitive-empathy#:~

Razzetti, G. (2019, March 11). *15 simple exercises to increase your self-awareness.* Fearless Culture. https://www.fearlessculture.design/blog-posts/15-simple-exercises-to-increase-your-self-awareness

Reid, S. (2023, October 11). *Empathy: how to feel and respond to the emotions of others.* HelpGuide.org. https://www.helpguide.org/articles/relationships-communication/empathy.htm#:~:

Richards, K. (2016, July 7). *Oprah's real secret to success may not be what you think it is.* Inc. https://www.inc.com/kelli-richards/oprah-s-real-secret-to-success-may-not-be-what-you-think-it-is.html

Rickardsson, J. (n.d.). *5 reasons why empathy is important in relationships.* 29k. https://29k.org/article/5-reasons-why-empathy-is-important-in-relationships

Riopel, L. (2019, September 14). *17 self-awareness activities and exercises (+ test).* Positive Psychology. https://positivepsychology.com/self-awareness-exercises-activities-test/

Roncero, A. (2021, February 12). *Empathetic leadership: are empathetic leaders born or made?* BetterUp. https://www.betterup.com/blog/empathetic-leadership

Salters-Pedneault, K. (2023). *What is impulsivity?* Verywell Mind. https://www.verywellmind.com/impulsive-behavior-and-bpd-425483

Schwantes, M. (2022, January 26). *Warren Buffett's lesson on emotional intelligence may be the best advice you will hear today.* Inc. https://www.inc.com/marcel-schwantes/warren-buffetts-lesson-on-emotional-intelligence-may-be-best-advice-you-will-hear-today.html

Scott, E. (2020). *5 self-care practices for every area of your life.* Verywell Mind. https://www.verywellmind.com/self-care-strategies-overall-stress-reduction-3144729

Scott, S. J. (2017, September 21). *33 self-awareness activities for adults and students.* Develop Good Habits. https://www.developgoodhabits.com/self-awareness-activities/

Segal, J. (2019a, August 12). *How to be emotionally intelligent in romantic relationships.* HelpGuide.org. https://www.helpguide.org/articles/mental-health/emotional-intelligence-love-relationships.htm

Segal, J. (2019b, August 12). *Tips to improve family relationships.* HelpGuide.org. https://www.helpguide.org/articles/mental-health/improving-family-relationships-with-emotional-intelligence.htm

Segal, J., Smith, M., Robinson, L., & Shubin, J. (2023, February 28). *Improving emotional intelligence (EQ).* HelpGuide.org. https://www.helpguide.org/articles/mental-health/emotional-intelligence-eq.htm

Shafner, E. (2019, December 23). *Practice the pause: 4 tips to become more mindful and have less conflict.* Imago Relationships North America. https://blog.

imagorelationshipswork.com/relationship-advice/become-more-mindful-have-less-conflict

Sharma, D. (2023, May 17). *5 ways emotional intelligence in communication helps you at work*. Risely. https://www.risely.me/ways-emotional-intelligence-in-communication-at-work/#:~

Silva Casablanca, S. (2014, June 8). *5 tips to be more empathetic in your relationship*. Psych Central. https://psychcentral.com/relationships/how-to-be-more-empathetic-in-relationship

Singhal, M. (2021, January 3). *6 things emotionally intelligent parents do differently*. Psychology Today. https://www.psychologytoday.com/intl/blog/the-therapist-mommy/202101/6-things-emotionally-intelligent-parents-do-differently#:~

Sobel, A. (2016, January 27). *Eight ways to improve your empathy*. Andrew Sobel. https://andrewsobel.com/article/eight-ways-to-improve-your-empathy/

Sutton, J. (2021, December 20). *7 stress-relief breathing exercises for calming your mind*. Positive Psychology. https://positivepsychology.com/breathing-exercises-for-stress-relief/

Thu-Huong, H. (2021, March 16). *5 exercises to help you build more empathy*. Ideas.ted.com. https://ideas.ted.com/5-exercises-to-help-you-build-more-empathy/

Verlinden, N. (2020, April 14). *Employee relations: examples + 10 strategy tips*. Academy to Innovate HR. https://www.aihr.com/blog/employee-relations/

Wagner, M. L. (n.d.). The power of apologies. In *Harvard Medical School*. https://hms.harvard.edu/sites/default/files/Departments/Ombuds%20Office/files/M.Wagner.ColumbiaUniversity.OmbudsOffice.ThePowerofApologies.pdf

What is emotional intelligence and 4 ways to improve it. (2018, November 15). Psychology Compass. https://psychologycompass.com/blog/what-is-emotional-intelligence/

What is team dynamics? Importance, key elements, and factors. (2023, April 21). ActiveCollab. https://activecollab.com/blog/collaboration/team-dynamics#:~

White, G. (2020, May 16). *Global leadership lessons from PepsiCo's Indra Nooyi*. Manufacturing. https://manufacturingdigital.com/smart-manufacturing/global-leadership-lessons-pepsicos-indra-nooyi

Williams, R. (2018, December 5). *Why Nelson Mandela was a great leader*. Ray Williams. https://raywilliams.ca/why-nelson-mandela-was-a-great-leader/

Wooll, M. (2021, July 1). *The importance of listening as a leader in the digital era*.

BetterUp. https://www.betterup.com/blog/the-importance-of-listening-as-a-leader-in-the-digital-era

Wooll, M. (2022a, February 24). *Developing the discipline of self-discipline.* BetterUp. https://www.betterup.com/blog/how-to-be-disciplined

Wooll, M. (2022b, August 26). *How to practice mindfulness and find peace from within.* BetterUp. https://www.betterup.com/blog/how-to-practice-mindfulness

Yamani, N., Shahabi, M., & Haghani, F. (2014). The relationship between emotional intelligence and job stress in the faculty of medicine in Isfahan University of Medical Sciences. *Journal of Advances in Medical Education & Professionalism, 2*(I), 20–26. https://www.ncbi.nlm.nih.gov/pmc/articles/PMC4235538/#:~:

Young, K. (2016, February 12). *9 ways to tap into your intuition (and why you'll want to).* Hey Sigmund. https://www.heysigmund.com/9-ways-to-tap-into-your-intuition-and-why-youll-want-to/

Yuen, C. (2018, November 29). *17 strategies for coping with stress in 30 minutes or less.* Healthline. https://www.healthline.com/health/mental-health/stress-coping-eliminate

Printed by Amazon Italia Logistica S.r.l.
Torrazza Piemonte (TO), Italy